Teacher's Guide
Grade 2

D1401110

Orlando   Austin   Chicago   New York   Toronto   London   San Diego

Visit *The Learning Site!*
www.harcourtschool.com

Printed in the United States of America

ISBN 0-15-334647-7

1 2 3 4 5 6 7 8 9 10   054   10 09 08 07 06 05 04 03 02

© Harcourt

Table of Contents

Building a Better Community

BACKGROUND

Summary

Beep, beep! Honking horns, skyscrapers, crowds, noise and pollution make up the picture we have of life in the city. But what about parks, trees, gardens and flowers? Today, in many cities, people are getting "back to nature." Communities come together and plant beautiful trees, flower beds and even vegetables that neighbors can weed, water, harvest and enjoy. One community garden blooms on the Lower East Side of New York City in what used to be a vacant lot. Students from the nearby high school take care of the garden—for school community service credit!

Though tall buildings dominate the city skyline, urban dwellers seem to cherish what countryfolk might take for granted. Nurturing a tomato plant in a roof garden, planting a strawberry plant in a window box, and hoeing a row of zucchini in a neighborhood garden can give many city people hours of pleasure. No matter how busy life is in the city, community gardens thrive because neighbors like working with nature, and with each other toward a common goal.

In Philadelphia, Pennsylvania, there is a non-profit group called the American Community Garden Association (A.C.G.A.). Their program, From the Roots Up, teaches groups around the United States how to start and maintain a community garden, especially in an urban area. The organization also answers gardening questions from local groups and supports grassroots efforts to create greenspaces.

FAST FACTS

- Community gardens began in New York City in the mid-1980s when old tenement buildings collapsed or burned down. After the city cleared the rubble from the land, vacant lots were left behind.

- Many of these projects in New York City have been deemed Operation GreenThumb (OGT). Neighbors lease the land from the city and get a permit to use it as a community garden. Artists in the Garden, an OGT program, commissions artists to create sculptures or to paint murals on garden walls.

- City gardens of the past, such as World War II victory gardens, provided much needed fresh fruit and vegetables during a time of food rationing. Today's community gardens raise a neighborhood's quality of life with flowers, vegetables, and art.

- Community gardens flourish around the country in cities like Atlanta, GA; Austin, TX; Idaho Falls, ID; Madison, WI; Philadelphia, PA; and Portland, OR.

- In Colorado, students aged 5 to 9 planted a Children's Peace Garden in North Boulder. They donate the food they grow to shelters for the homeless in the community.

- A completely organic community garden in South Austin, TX, supplies fruits and vegetables for its volunteers and for the local Salvation Army's soup kitchen.

READING TIPS

Before Reading

- Talk about neighborhoods. What kind of neighborhood do your students live in? What makes an area a neighborhood (a grouping of homes, stores, hospital, library, etc.)? What makes their neighborhood special?
- Expand on children's sense of neighborhood to introduce the word *community* (basically, a group of neighborhoods) and the common goal of keeping the area enjoyable for everyone. Talk about civic pride, a community's positive sense of itself.
- Ask if children have ever helped plant a garden. What do they think is involved?

■ It's amazing what you can plant in a small space. Some of the flowers and vegetables in a city's community garden include tomatoes, peppers, broccoli, cabbages, apples, pears, strawberries, petunias, hollyhocks, daisies, snapdragons, roses and pansies.

Critical Thinking

■ Talk about what children might find in a city neighborhood. What does it look like? List the descriptions on the left of the chalkboard. On the right, talk about a suburban neighborhood, or a rural setting. What are the similarities? the differences?

■ Whatever occurs in a community affects everyone living there. Members of a community affect their neighborhood and have a say in how things work. Talk about what it means to get involved in your local community, and how the people in this story turned an empty lot into a beautiful garden. Without dedication and hard work, this would not have happened.

■ In this book, each gardener has a plot to maintain. A community garden means that each member has a say, or a vote, in making decisions that affect the garden. If one person lets his or her plot go unattended, it affects the entire garden. Before signing up, people need to agree to go to monthly meetings about the garden and to give time—for example, an hour a week—for whatever needs doing. Everyone has to pitch in and help.

■ Community gardens have a positive effect on neighborhoods. They help improve the quality of life, and crime rates go down. Residents have more pride in where they live. Children, too, have a nicer place to play.

Activities

■ Imagine a perfect neighborhood. What would it include? Perhaps an ice-cream stand on every corner? Flowers everywhere? Ramps for skateboarding? A slide next to every group of stairs? Be creative and imaginative; this is fiction, after all. Make a list together as a class.

■ Now, be realistic. Ask children to think about things in their community that may need fixing. Perhaps a playground has fallen into disrepair, a mall needs a wheelchair ramp, or there is a broken statue in the middle of town. Brainstorm ideas to make your community better. Write a letter to a local elected official with your suggestions.

EXTENSION ACTIVITIES

LOOKING AT PHOTOGRAPHS
What do you like best about the garden?

COMMUNITY CLUES
Skills: Critical Thinking, Memory, Current Events
Curriculum Area: Social Studies
Play a guessing game. Have children take turns describing places in their community. Classmates have to guess the location. It can be as easy as "there's a bunch of mailboxes in the front" or "it has the best pizza in town, but you can never find a parking space."

COMMUNITY FEELINGS
Skills: Exploring Emotions, Current Events
Curriculum Area: Social Studies
A community has an essence, or a feel about it. It makes an impression. Discuss with children their feelings about their community. What do they like? dislike? What makes the community famous (a winning team, a great restaurant, a skating pond)? When is the community most enjoyable? annoying? How would you change the community if you could? Use the copying master "My Favorite Place" to draw a special place in your community.

ANSWER KEY

COPYING MASTER
Page 3 my house; backyard; toy store; playground; beach; museum.

READER
Think and Respond **1.** The community garden was planted in an empty lot. **2.** People plant them to grow food and flowers and to beautify their communities. **3.** Possible responses: I would plant flowers, vegetables, trees, grass.

Draw Pictures Children's drawings should show an area in their community as it is now and as it would look if people work to improve it. Children's sentences should describe their drawings.

© Harcourt

My Favorite Place

Where do you like to go in your community? Unscramble the names of these places. Then draw a picture of your favorite one, and explain why this place is your favorite.

ym sheou _____

ybcakrad _____

yto erost _____

lapydrgoun_____

cheab _____

umuesm_____

Name_____

My Community Hero

Is there someone in your community who makes a difference in your life? Who helps you to be a better person or to see another's point of view? That kind of person is a role model, someone you admire and who cares about you. Write a letter to your role model. Tell that person why you think he or she is important.

Dear _____,

You are my role model in the community because

_____

_____

_____

_____

_____

_____

Love,

_____

BUILDING A BETTER COMMUNITY

Amelia Earhart

© Harcourt

BACKGROUND

Summary

Are you brave? Are you adventurous? Do you like to take risks? If so, you have some of the traits of Amelia Earhart, the first woman to fly across the Atlantic Ocean by herself. She was a go-getter, eager to take chances, and willing to work hard. She was also a bit of a tomboy. She was born on July 24, 1897 and grew up in the days when women were not always encouraged to work outside the home, let alone fly airplanes! Amelia Earhart defied the critics. She went to medical school and then took up flying, encouraging other women along the way. Her famous solo flight occurred in 1931. That only led her to try harder to break other records. On March 17, 1937 she took off again, to do what no one had done before: circle the equator by plane. A man named Fred Noonan accompanied her as navigator. Both were wary of the new devices equipping the plane, such as a radio transmitter. In fact, when they took off from Oakland, California, the team left the transmitter behind. In the end, that might have been a crucial mistake. High above Howland Island, in the Pacific Ocean, her plane disappeared, never to be found. Perhaps if someone had remembered the radio, the outcome might have been different. Today, many theories and mysteries surround her final moments.

FAST FACTS

■ In 1921 Amelia Earhart scraped together enough money to buy her first plane.

■ Because Amelia Earhart believed that women should follow their careers, she helped establish an organization of woman pilots called the Ninety-Nines.

■ Amelia almost always wore her flying gear: boots, khaki pants, a knee-length flying jacket, and a scarf around her neck.

■ To keep herself awake on long flights, Amelia packed smelling salts along with a thermos of soup and a can of tomato juice.

■ At one point in her flying career, the press dubbed Earhart "Lady Lindy," a female Charles Lindbergh.

■ In 1931 she married George Palmer Putnam, of a large publishing family. At one point she was even the aviation editor of *Cosmopolitan* magazine.

■ In August 1932 Earhart flew from Los Angeles, California, to Newark, New Jersey. It took 19 hours and 15 minutes—the fastest time for a woman.

■ Ten pilots before her had already lost their lives trying to complete a trans-Pacific flight. Amelia's would be the first in which a civilian plane carried a two-way radio telephone.

READING TIPS

Before Reading

■ Amelia Earhart was born in Atchison, Kansas, in 1897, the first of two daughters. Her sister, Muriel, was born three years later. Amy Otis Earhart and Edwin Earhart encouraged their daughters to experience whatever they wanted. They even allowed the girls to wear pants!

■ The Earhart girls grew up amid wealth and privilege. They went to private school and enjoyed many of the comforts of life. Do children think that this environment, plus Amelia's parents' "go for it" attitude, gave Amelia strength and confidence in herself?

■ Her life changed when her father started drinking and losing various jobs (he was a lawyer); Amy and Edwin got a divorce when Amelia was in high school. Talk about how difficult this might have been for her. Ask: Can bad experiences make you stronger?

Critical Thinking

■ After accompanying her family to some stunt-plane shows, Amelia was hooked on flying! After many years with no idea of what she wanted to do, now she knew. Ask: Do any of you know what you want to do when you grow up? Who inspires you?

■ Amelia became the first woman to fly solo across the Atlantic Ocean because George Palmer Putnam, the author of a book about the famous aviator Charles Lindbergh, chose her for this flight. Her eagerness and her growing knowledge of planes influenced his decision. Discuss how your attitude can make a difference.

■ At the time of Earhart's flight, many people feared flying, especially women. Ask: Why do you think flying might have been scary?

■ Discuss what it means to beat a record. Do Olympic athletes break records? What other achievers have broken records?

Activities

■ Amelia Earhart's first love was the airplane. Write down three things you love to do or to learn about.

■ Earhart took chances. Ask: What have you done that's challenging? Discuss this as a class, and then have children draw a picture of a time when they were daring.

■ Brainstorm the names of other great women of our time, and what made them famous.

EXTENSION ACTIVITIES

LOOKING AT PHOTOGRAPHS

Why do you think Amelia Earhart loved to fly?

GREAT WOMEN

Skills: Cognitive Thinking, Research, Writing
Curriculum Areas: Social Studies, Language Arts
Discuss how different — and in some cases, difficult — life in the 19th century was for women. Have

children research some of the women behind the women's equal rights movement, including Elizabeth Cady Stanton, Lucretia Mott, Susan B. Anthony and others. Point out how Amelia Earhart not only broke aviation records, but also changed the public's perception of what women could and could not do. She followed her dreams, and never let go. Use the copying master "Letter to Amelia" to have students write a letter to Amelia Earhart.

DREAM TO TRAVEL

Skill: Current Events
Curriculum Areas: Social Studies, Language Arts
Amelia Earhart was flying a twin-engine Lockheed Electra on her last journey. That meant she could not move, stand or stretch in the cockpit. It was that small—about the size of a doghouse. Yet she loved it. Where would you like to visit and explore? Use copying master "Exploring!" to write where you'd like to travel to, and why. (It has to be someplace you've never been but have heard about!)

ANSWER KEY

READER

Think and Respond 1. Neta Snook taught Amelia how to fly. 2. Amelia's achievements were special because she was the first woman to do them. 3. Possible responses: What do you like so much about flying? How does it feel to break records? Do you have any advice for girls?

Measure Distances Children should find the locations on a map and use the map scale to determine the distances from Harbor Grace, Newfoundland, to Londonderry, Northern Ireland—approximately 2,026 miles (3,260 km)—and from Los Angeles, California, to Newark, New Jersey—approximately 2,448 miles (3,940 km).

Letter to Amelia

Write to Amelia Earhart. Tell her why you think that she deserves to be in the National Women's Hall of Fame.

Dear Amelia:

_____

_____

_____

_____

_____

_____

_____

_____

From

_____

Exploring!

What place would you like to go to that you've never been to before? Think about it, write about it, and draw a picture.

I'd like to visit _____ because

_____

_____

_____

_____ .

Here is a picture of what I would do if I visited there.

AMELIA EARHART

Living in Athens

BACKGROUND

Summary

Standing in the center of modern Athens, it's not hard to imagine Greece in its golden age, more than 2,500 years ago. Simply gaze up at the towering Parthenon, perched on the city's highest point, the Acropolis. Close your eyes and picture this. You're walking through the marketplace, or agora, on your way to the gymnasium for your morning exercise. As you pass by the courthouse, you hear two fellow Athenians arguing a point of law.

That reminds you that tonight you're going to see "The Flea," a new play at the outdoor theater by a young man named Aristophanes. As usual it will be performed by an all-male cast. You wish that you could bring your sister Athena, but women may not attend the theater. At the gymnasium, you slip off your leather-strap sandals and toga to take a swim. If you get strong enough, maybe you can enter the games at Olympia this year. It's wonderful to live in the greatest city-state in the world!

FAST FACTS

■ Athens was the center of Greek civilization and culture, attracting many famous playwrights, such as Aristophanes, and thinkers, such as Socrates and Plato.

■ In its classical period (500–350 B.C.), Greece consisted of city-states, with Athens as its largest. Each city-state had high walls around it, an agora (marketplace), and a fort (acropolis) at its highest point.

■ The agora served as the center of political life. An acropolis was the religious center of each city-state.

■ Painted scenes on ancient Greek pottery give us a glimpse into ancient life. They also show many of the gods the Greeks worshipped.

■ The second major city-state was Sparta, a military center. Male Spartans began military training at the age of 7 and remained soldiers until they were 60.

■ Theater began in Athens as a singing and acting festival to honor the god Dionysus.

■ All the actors in ancient Greece were men; they acted the female parts as well.

■ Athens will host the 2004 Olympic Games.

READING TIPS

Before Reading

■ Set the stage! Men had the power in Greece. Families were not always happy when a girl was born. In fact, when a baby arrived, its father decided whether the family would keep it or abandon it. Unwanted babies were left in the open air to die. Sometimes they were saved by other families and brought up as slaves.

■ Boys were taught to be good soldiers; physical exercise was very important to ancient Greeks.

■ The Olympics originated in Greece; they were held in Olympia every four years in honor of Zeus. Male athletes came from all over Greece to compete. No women were allowed to participate.

■ Music played an important role in Greek life. There were songs for every occasion— births, weddings, funerals, battles, and harvest time. Musical instruments included the harp, the lyre, and the kithara (a kind of lyre). Greek men did not dance; dancing was for women.

■ Greek theater was different from the theater we know. Performed in open-air coliseums, plays with all-male casts featured a chorus, which would comment on the play's actions and address the audience directly. Music accompanied the plays. It is believed that women were not allowed to attend the theater.

■ Discuss how many of our sports facilities are modeled after ancient Greek structures, as are many theaters and temples. Many of our words, our ideas, our buildings and our sources of entertainment have roots in ancient Greece.

Critical Thinking

■ Ask: Is l2 or l3 really a good age to leave school? Was a Greek childhood as "easy" as a childhood today? Would you be so quick to give up your toys?
■ Did ancient Greece treat men and women equally? boys and girls? Would you rather have been a boy or a girl in ancient Greece?

Activities

■ Reread the book. Then ask: How would you spend your days as a child in ancient Greece? (go to school if a boy; do housework if a girl; enjoy music if a girl, play sports if a boy)
■ Ask: Would your clothing be the same as today? Have children draw pictures of themselves wearing ancient Greek clothing.

EXTENSION ACTIVITIES

LOOKING AT PHOTOGRAPHS

Does Athens look like an interesting place to visit? Why?

WRITE A MYTH!

Skills: Imagination, Writing
Curriculum Area: Language Arts

The ancient Greeks used myths to explain many natural events: lightning was created by the all-powerful god Zeus, and the sun was a flaming chariot driven across the sky by the god Helios.

Ask children to think of something in nature that they have wondered about. For example, why is the sky blue? Why does the wind blow? Why does the moon look larger and smaller during a month? Invite children to use their imaginations, and to create a myth-like story that provides an answer to their question. Have children share their myths with classmates.

GREECE TODAY

Skill: Current Events
Curriculum Areas: Social Studies, Geography

Discuss Greek society today. What is life there like now? Talk about how Athens is a bustling metropolitan center, with awesome ruins that are reminders of its great past. What kinds of food do people in Greece eat? What is the weather like? What time is it there now? What kinds of jobs do people have? What is life like for children? What language(s) do people speak? Have children do research to find out the answers to these questions. How does what they find out about life today compare with what they know about life in ancient Greece? Use the copying master "Then and Now" to record differences and spark discussion.

ANSWER KEY

COPYING MASTER

Page 12 **1.** Ancient: boys only until age 12; Modern: boys and girls K–12. **2.** Ancient: chiton; Modern: jeans, t-shirts. **3.** Ancient: lyre; Modern: all instruments. **4.** Ancient: all–male outdoor theater; Modern: TV, computers, plays with both men and women. **5.** Ancient: Olympic games; Modern: Olympic games.

READER

Think and Respond **1.** Athens is in Greece. **2.** We have plays and outdoor theaters, musical instruments, and the Olympic Games. **3.** Possible responses: I would like to have lived in ancient Greece because I like the clothes people wore; I would like to have seen the Parthenon when it was new.

Write about a Building Children should select a building discussed in the Reader and should write a paragraph about it. Children's paragraphs should explain why they think the place is special and why they would like to visit it.

Name_____

Connect-the-Dots
Constellation

The ancient Greeks used myths to explain how the stars came into existence. Connect the dots to see the constellation of Pegasus, the flying horse.

© Harcourt

Name_____

Then and Now

TIME FOR KIDS READERS
COPYING MASTER

What was life like in Ancient Athens? How is it different—or the same—in Athens today? Re-read the book and use the library to complete the chart below.

	Ancient Athens	Modern Athens
1. Education		
2. Clothing		
3. Musical Instruments		
4. Entertainment		
5. Sports		

© Harcourt

We Elect a President

BACKGROUND

Summary

As students grow up, parents and teachers give them more privileges and responsibilities. They might have to do chores, such as walking the dog or baby-sitting. But what's the most powerful privilege American students gain just by turning 18? It's the right to vote for President—to cast a ballot and make their voices heard.

We elect a new President every four years. Presidential candidates must be American-born and at least 35 years old. They must have lived in the United States for at least 14 years. Candidates campaign hard, traveling all over the United States, meeting as many people as they can. Their platforms, or ideas for running the nation, reflect their party's beliefs.

Election Day is the first Tuesday after the first Monday in November. However, that day's vote—called the popular vote—is only one-half of the presidential election process. The Electoral College—a body in which the number of members from each state equals the sum of its senators and representatives—makes the deciding vote. For each state that a candidate wins by the popular vote, he or she also earns its Electoral College votes. The candidate with the most Electoral College votes wins. The 538 members of the Electoral College have so much power that their vote can stall the outcome of an election. During the last presidential election, the nation waited and waited while election officials investigated problems with Florida's popular vote. Why? Because Florida's 27 electoral votes would decide the next President! In 2000, the winner was George W. Bush.

READING TIPS

Before Reading

■ Because we live in a democracy, the population votes and has a say in choosing who fulfills the country's wants and needs at the government level. The word *democracy* comes from the ancient Greek words *demos* meaning "people" and *kratia* meaning "power."

■ Discuss the electoral process. Use the 2000 election as a starting point. Can a candidate who didn't win the popular vote still win a majority of the electoral votes? Yes! That's what happened between Al Gore and George W. Bush in November 2000; Bush won the electoral vote; Gore won the popular vote. A candidate needs at least 270 electoral votes to win.

■ Talk about a President's responsibilities. The President heads the executive branch of the federal government. He is responsible for enforcing the laws passed by Congress and is commander in chief of the United States Armed Forces.

Critical Thinking

■ Candidates Gore and Bush weren't the only ones with a close race. In 1876 Samuel Tilden won a majority of the popular vote but lost the election to

---

FAST FACTS

■ No president can be elected more than twice.

■ If the president dies or cannot complete his term, the vice president takes over. The next person in line to serve is the Speaker of the House of Representatives.

■ George Washington chose the site for the president's house, at 1600 Pennsylvania Avenue, but John Adams was the first president to live there.

■ Our longest-serving President was Franklin D. Roosevelt; he lived in the White House for 12 years, from 1933 to 1945.

■ A presidential candidate needs 270 electoral college votes to win the election.

Rutherford Hayes by one electoral vote; in 1888 Grover Cleveland won the popular vote but lost to Benjamin Harrison, who won the Electoral College votes. Discuss: Is the Electoral College a good idea?

■ Discuss: Why would someone want to be President? Is it an easy job? Or difficult?

■ How many Presidents have we had so far? George W. Bush is our forty-third president. Ask if anyone can name his Vice President. (Dick Cheney) Ask: What other Presidents stick out in your mind, and for what reason? (George Washington, for being the first; Abraham Lincoln, for freeing the slaves; John F. Kennedy, for his promise to send an American to the moon, etc.)

Activities

■ Ask children to name our last four (most recent) Presidents. Ask: Who was President when you were born? Who was Vice President? Then share which President served when you were born (and let students do the math!).

■ The President has a busy schedule every day. What is your daily schedule? Write down what you do on a typical school day and on a Saturday or Sunday. Be sure to include the times you start and finish each item on your schedule. Are you a busy person? Does writing a schedule help you remember what to do?

■ What would be an important thing you'd like to do if you were elected President? Brainstorm ideas with the class and ways to achieve these goals.

EXTENSION ACTIVITIES

LOOKING AT PHOTOGRAPHS

Why is it important to vote?

WHAT'S YOUR PLATFORM?
Skills: Critical Thinking, Current Events
Curriculum Area: Social Studies

What would children do if they were elected to public office? Every candidate has a platform—ideas he or she would like to see implemented if elected. Each idea is one "plank" of the platform. Have children break into two groups. Ask: What would you

do to improve our community? Ask them to list these ideas on the copying master "My Political Platform" and to share them with the class. How do the two groups' ideas differ? How are they the same?

POSTER POWER
Skills: Research, Current Events
Curriculum Area: Social Studies

Every time there's an election, candidates create posters to advertise themselves. Sometimes these posters feature a picture of the candidate working in the community or have a catchy phrase or slogan. First, have children research the slogans of presidential candidates and share them with the class. Discuss: What makes a slogan easy to remember? Have each child create a poster advertising him- or herself for President. Use the copying master "Vote for Me" as the basis for the poster.

ANSWER KEY

READER

Think and Respond 1. To be President, you must be born a United States citizen, you must have lived in the United States for 14 years or more, and you must be at least 35 years old. 2. Possible responses: At 18, you are grown up enough to make good decisions about our nation's leaders. At 35, you have enough experience in life to be a good President. 3. Possible responses: I would like to be President someday because I think I can make the world a more peaceful place and help keep the environment clean.

Draw a Poster Children's posters should reflect an understanding of what makes a good President.

Name____

My Political Platform

TIME FOR KIDS READERS
COPYING MASTER

What are your ideas to make your community a better place to live? Write each idea below. When you have filled all 5, you have a platform.

What I Would Do to Improve:

Education ____

Business ____

Parks ____

Laws ____

Town Pride ____

Name____

Vote for Me!

TIME FOR KIDS READERS
COPYING MASTER

You're running for President! Make a poster telling people about you and your ideas.

My Name:

____

____

____

My Slogan:

____

____

____

____

____

Why You Should Vote for Me:

____

____

____

____

Paul Revere and Historic Boston

BACKGROUND

Summary

Silently the shadowy figure gazed across the river. He peered toward the belfry of Old North Church. Through the midnight murk he made out one lantern, and then another. "One if by land, two if by sea...." The signal had come, and he leapt onto his steed.

"The British are coming, the British are coming!" So yelled the rider, silversmith Paul Revere, on the night of April 18, 1775. From Charlestown, Massachusetts, Revere rode to Lexington in the middle of the night to warn his fellow colonists. The two lamps meant that the attack would come by water. As Revere galloped, the British warship *Somerset* floated in Boston Harbor. Colonial troops now knew where the enemy was and the battle began.

FAST FACTS

■ Born in 1734, Paul Revere was the second of at least 9 and possibly 12 children; he was the oldest son.

■ Paul Revere's house is the oldest in Boston, dating to 1680. Paul Revere owned it from 1770 to 1800. Today, it is a museum furnished as it was when Revere lived there.

■ History does not tell us the name of Paul Revere's horse. It is believed he borrowed one named Brown Beauty from John Larkin.

■ The Freedom Trail takes you from Boston Commons to the berth of the U.S.S. *Constitution*.

■ The Old North Church was built in 1723 as a house for prayer for all people. Today it is known as "Old North" or Christ Church and is the city's oldest church.

■ Paul Revere died at age 83; he is buried in Boston's Granary Burying Ground.

Revere's ride launched the American Revolution, when the 13 colonies fought for independence from Britain. Tension had been building for months, due to what the colonists believed were unfair taxes and unfair laws. The war lasted from 1775 to 1783. Today, there are parts of Boston where this history comes alive. Some of the main attractions include the Freedom Trail, a 2½-mile walk marked with red bricks, passing some of Boston's most famous landmarks in the fight for independence. It includes the Old South Meeting House, built in 1729, where Boston colonists met to protest British rule. You can even visit Paul Revere's house.

READING TIPS

Before Reading

■ Point out Boston on a map; discuss some other places of historic significance, such as the Boston Commons, once a cow pasture and later used as a training field for soldiers in the American Revolution.

■ Revere was politically connected; he was friendly with many activists and some were even his business clients, so he was eager to help when the call came. His friend Dr. Joseph Warren asked him to ride to Lexington, Massachusetts, to warn Samuel Adams and John Hancock that the British troops were on their way.

Critical Thinking

■ Talk about the deep emotions of the people living in Revolutionary Boston during the American Revolution, and tell children that the colonists were willing to go to war to gain liberty. Ask: Is freedom worth fighting for? What does it mean to be patriotic?

■ Paul Revere married Sarah Orne in 1757 and had eight children. After Sarah died in 1773, he married Rachel Walker and had eight more children! Explain that large families were usual back then. Ask: Would you like to have eight or more brothers and sisters? What are some differences between large families and small ones?

Activities

■ The colonists used lanterns as signals. Think of other signals we use today. (e.g., traffic lights, stop signs, walk signs, flags at half-mast). Brainstorm as a class.

■ Aside from being a key figure during the Revolution, Paul Revere was also a father. What does your dad, stepfather or grandfather do that makes you proud?

EXTENSION ACTIVITIES

LOOKING AT PHOTOGRAPHS

If you visited historic Boston, what would you want to see first?

POETIC JUSTICE

Skill: Listening
Curriculum Area: Language Arts

Read children the famous Henry Wadsworth Longfellow poem, "Paul Revere's Ride," and then ask: What kind of man was Paul Revere? Would you have taken the same risks he did? Then have children think about the use of poetry to describe a dramatic event. Ask: What kinds of feelings does this poem give you? Invite children to use the copying master "What Freedom Means to Me" to write poems.

UNDERSTANDING GOALS

Skill: Cognitive Thinking
Curriculum Area: Social Studies

Our forefathers had dreams for this country that they had to fight for. Talk about what it means to have goals. What are some long-term goals? What are some short-term goals? Discuss the differences, explaining why it's important to have both. Ask: What are your goals?

MAP IT OUT

Skills: Mapping, Current Events
Curriculum Area: Social Studies

Take a virtual walk with your students on Boston's Freedom trail. Begin by using the Web to print out a map. Then "walk" and see the sights, including Park Street Church/Granary Burying Ground, where Paul Revere is buried. Other important people are buried there too, including Declaration of Independence signers John Hancock, Robert Treat Paine and Samuel Adams. Talk about the Old South Meeting House, built in 1729 as a Congregational Church but also used as a town meeting site for large groups. Its most famous meeting took place on December 16, 1773, when Bostonians met to consider the new British tax on tea. Old South remained a church until the 1870s. The Old State House was the seat of colonial government; the Boston Massacre took place there on March 5, 1770, when British soldiers killed five patriots. Quincy Market is now a bustling shopping and eating area on the waterfront, as is Faneuil Hall. The second-floor meeting hall was dubbed the "Cradle of Liberty" because many protests against British policy were held there. Ask: What's your favorite place on the Freedom Trail? Which stop would you like to learn more about?

ANSWER KEY

READER

Think and Respond **1.** Revere is famous because he warned colonial troops that the British were about to attack. **2.** Boston is interesting to visit because many of the buildings where history was made still stand today. **3.** Possible responses: I would have done the same as Revere; I would have been scared and asked a friend to go with me.

Research Your Community's History Children should research a statue, monument, or building that reflects something important to the community. They should find out where the object is located, when it was made, and what it signifies.

Name_____

What Freedom Means to Me

Citizens of the United States today are proud of the bravery of Paul Revere. Many times throughout United States history, people have taken risks and taken daring actions because they loved their country. Answer these questions about freedom. Share your answers.

What does it mean to be brave?

_____

_____

_____

What does it mean to live in a free country?

_____

_____

_____

What does it mean to be patriotic?

_____

_____

A Letter to a Friend

Pretend that you are a friend of Paul Revere's. You know about his plan and would like to help him succeed. Write a letter to your friend, letting him know why you think his mission is so important and valuable.

Dear Paul,

    I want you to know how proud I am to be your friend today. Your mission to warn our troops about the British is important because _____

_____

_____

_____

_____.

Be brave, my friend!

        Sincerely,

        _____

© Harcourt

PAUL REVERE, HISTORIC BOSTON

BACKGROUND

Summary

Tigers...they're the largest and toughest of the big cats on this planet. Incredibly powerful predators, Bengal tigers can bring down wild cattle weighing a ton or more. They are as agile as they are strong: tigers can leap more than 30 feet in a single bound, climb trees, and swim for miles. And in their forest habitats, they can instantly disappear into the brush.

Today, because of pollution, forest clearing and development, tigers and many other animals around the world are at risk. The word that describes tigers and other threatened species says it best: endangered. Right in the center of that word there's a warning that humans must heed: DANGER.

Right now, big trees in the Amazon Rain Forest are being chopped down; oceans and the sealife that lives in them are being polluted with our waste. We are destroying habitats—environments that support wildlife—at an alarming rate. We have to work together now—cooperate—and conserve resources to protect our fragile environment for the future.

FAST FACTS

■ Rain forests are fragile. If one is cleared, it takes hundreds of years to "reforest" the same area.

■ Rain forests have been evolving for 70 to 100 million years. They contain unique plants and animals that don't exist elsewhere.

■ Plant and animal species are disappearing at least 1,000 times faster than at any other time in the last 65 million years.

■ Only about 5,000 to 7,000 tigers live in the wild today.

■ Wildlife conservation has become one of the most important jobs of zoos today. Zoos breed many endangered species to increase their numbers.

READING TIPS

Before Reading

■ Explain the word habitat (where animals live). A good habitat provides water, food and shelter for animals.

■ Talk about *endangered species* (animals that are few in number). Hunting laws and endangered species lists protect some animals. But nations need to agree to limit activities like forest-clearing and to set up pollution controls. Ask: What other steps might help?

Critical Thinking

■ Why are some animals and plants becoming extinct? Because humans are taking up more and more space and destroying their habitats. Ask: What do humans do? (Build homes, malls, and gas stations) We also pollute the world's oceans, making survival difficult for creatures of the sea.

■ Brainstorm ways people can help, such as becoming a volunteer at a zoo, learning about caring for plants and animals and recycling waste.

Activities

■ "Adopt" an endangered animal. Is it the cute and cuddly panda? Or the large rhino? Find out more about an animal and efforts to protect it.

■ Write a letter to your local zoo, asking if they house endangered animals. Which ones do they have? How do they care for them? Do they hope to put them back into the wild? Think of other questions you'd like to ask a zookeeper.

EXTENSION ACTIVITIES

LOOKING AT PHOTOGRAPHS
Why do we need to protect our environment?

ENDANGERED ANIMALS
Skill: Current Events
Curriculum Area: Social Studies

Ask children to brainstorm animals they think might be endangered. Re-read the book for clues. The list includes Indian elephants (in South-central and southeast Asia), blue whales (all oceans), giant pandas (China), snow leopards (Central Asia), tigers (Southern Asia, China, Eastern Russia), the American crocodile (Florida, Mexico, Central and South America, Caribbean islands), the black rhinoceros (South of Sahara in Africa) and the red wolf (Southeastern U.S.) to name a few. Our earth supports a lot of plant and animal species, but with more and more humans changing the environment, species are becoming extinct a lot faster.

DISCUSSION: ACTIVISM
Skills: Current Events, Cognitive Thinking
Curriculum Area: Social Studies

What is an *activist*? (Someone who's involved in raising awareness about certain issues and making plans to solve those problems.) Discuss things you can do in your area and how you can make a difference. Plan a playground/schoolyard clean-up day. Organize your class to make it a better, cleaner place for you and the birds, bugs and other small creatures that live there. Find out about the National Wildlife Federation's EarthSavers Club. Then start an EarthSavers Club for people who want to learn more about the environment and make this planet a better place.

ANSWER KEY

COPYING MASTER
Page 23 **1.** panda, **2.** tiger, **3.** elephant, **4.** bald eagle

READER
Think and Respond **1.** Some animal habitats disappear because people take up more space on Earth, or because people destroy the habitats. **2.** People work to keep the environment clean and support zoos that care for endangered animals. **3.** It is a good idea to protect endangered species because they cannot protect themselves. They are endangered because of what people have done to the environment.

Write a Report Children's reports should be about an endangered animal and should include five facts about it.

WORKING TOGETHER TO SAVE OUR PLANET

Animal Name Game

1. I am famous for looking loveable. My home was destroyed in China when bamboo forests were cleared for rice farms. Who am I?

_____

2. I am the largest cat in the world. If you saw me, you'd be seeing stripes! Who am I?

_____

3. Hunters in Africa kill me for my ivory tusks, which are used to make jewelry. Who am I?

_____

4. I'm "America's bird" and thousands of me used to fill our nation's skies. Now I live in the Northwest, but also appear on a U.S. coin. Who am I?

_____

Name_____

An Animal I Like

Choose an animal you like. It can be at the zoo or in your home. Learn about it. Draw a picture of it. Then write a report about it. Use these questions to write your report.

What kind of animal is it?

_____

If it has a name, what is it?

_____

When was it born? Where?

_____

Where does it live?

_____

What does it eat?

_____

What makes this animal special to you?

_____

_____

_____

WORKING TOGETHER TO SAVE OUR PLANET

Sun Power

TIME FOR KIDS READERS

BACKGROUND

Summary

Born about five billion years ago from a cloud of hydrogen and helium mixed with dust, this mighty glowing orb is Earth's best friend. Its energy warms our atmosphere, helps create the weather, and sustains life on our planet, and that's just the beginning. What do we call such a powerful star? The sun.

The sun is actually a star, but its effect on Earth far exceeds that of the others that twinkle in the night sky. Why? Because it is so close to Earth that its energy affects our atmosphere. And we're not the only sphere in the sky influenced by the sun. In our part of the universe, in our solar system, all nine planets (including Earth) travel around the sun.

Meanwhile, back on Earth, the Sun nourishes plant life, which provides the food that people and animals eat. The sun's warmth creates different climates and also changes in weather. Life on Earth wouldn't exist without the sun's energy. Scientists "collect" that power to provide heat and electricity. They place solar panels on roofs, on mountain peaks and in other locations with steady sunlight. The panels absorb the sun's energy and convert it into electricity. Solar power can be used to start the engines of cars or flick on the lights in a house. Solar power is called a 'clean' form of energy because using it does not pollute our planet. It's likely that researchers will discover many exciting ways to harness solar power in the years to come.

FAST FACTS

■ The sun provides the light and heat that sustains all life on Earth.

■ Scientists believe the sun will continue to shine for another five billion years before it runs out of hydrogen fuel and begins to die.

■ The moon does not give off its own light: it is bright only because, like a mirror, it reflects light from the sun.

■ The sun gives off more energy in one second than humans have produced in all of history.

■ Earth is the third planet from the sun.

■ The sun is the center of our solar system.

■ The sun is just one of millions of stars in the Milky Way.

READING TIPS

Before Reading

■ The sun is really a giant ball of gases, mostly hydrogen, and Earth's greatest energy source. In a complicated process known as nuclear fusion, its hydrogen is converted to helium and then rises to the sun's surface in the form of waves. These waves give us heat and light. The sun's energy is also stored in our food, which provides fuel for our bodies. So, in essence, we need the sun as much as plants and animals do, to grow.

■ Discuss the topic of energy. Energy sustains and refreshes all life forms, including people. Ask: Do you feel more tired on days when the sun is hidden behind clouds? Do you feel more energetic when it's a nice sunny day? The sun gives us energy.

■ Explain that the sun is a natural resource; it is not something man-made.

Critical Thinking

■ Brainstorm: What are some ways your family could conserve energy? (turn the lights off when you leave a room; turn off the TV when you're not watching, and so on.)

■ Discuss: Why has our energy use increased? Did your parents have microwaves when they were young? VCRs? DVD players? A TV in each room? Or computers? We use power sources every day without really thinking about it.

■ Ask: Have you had a sunburn? The sun's power can sometimes take you by surprise. Invisible ultraviolet (UV) rays penetrate our skin. Serious sunburns can cause premature aging of the skin and sometimes lead to skin cancer. This is why you need to wear sunscreen and use sunglasses.

Activities

■ Keep a "sunny mood" chart. Note sunny days on the class calendar or use the copying master "Let the Sun Shine In," and poll students to see if energy levels rise on sunny days.

■ Why is it a good idea to protect yourself from the sun? List as many ways as you can think of to stay safe in the sun.

■ What are some other energy sources? Brainstorm as a class.

EXTENSION ACTIVITIES

LOOKING AT PHOTOGRAPHS

How does the sun's energy turn into electricity?

AN "OPPOSITE" DAY

Skills: Creativity, Imagination
Curriculum Area: Social Studies

If we didn't have the sun, life would be topsy-turvy. Make an "Opposite Day" in your classroom. Create an "afternoon to morning" schedule for the day by brainstorming as a class, and then follow this schedule. At the end (beginning?) of the day, ask children how they feel about the reverse schedule. How was it different from an ordinary day?

DISCUSSION: THE SOLAR SYSTEM

Skills: Current Events, Vocabulary
Curriculum Area: Social Studies

Introduce the planets of the solar system (in order from the Sun: Mercury, Venus, Earth, Mars, Jupiter, Saturn, Uranus, Neptune, Pluto) and the moon. Look together at pictures of the solar system. Encourage children to choose a planet and find out more about it. Talk about how Earth is the only planet in our solar system that supports life. However, there are millions of other stars like our sun that may or may not have planets with life forms. Ask: Do you think other planets have life forms? Also use this opportunity to introduce some new words: *atmosphere* (a layer of air); *gravity* (the invisible force that holds us on Earth); *astronauts* (the people who go into space and study it); the *Milky Way* (the galaxy that contains our sun and billions of other stars); and *universe* (the name we give to space and everything in it).

ANSWER KEY

COPYING MASTER

Page 27 **1.** Mercury, **2.** Venus, **3.** Earth, **4.** Mars, **5.** Jupiter, **6.** Saturn, **7.** Uranus, **8.** Neptune, **9.** Pluto

READER

Think and Respond **1.** The sun warms the land, the water, and people. **2.** People use the sun's power to heat homes, and to make cars, watches and other machines work. **3.** Possible responses: Use sun power because it's free, it's clean and it's not bad for the environment.

Grow Plants Children's drawings should accurately show what the plants look like now. Children's observations should reflect the understanding that a plant kept in sunlight will grow more rapidly than a plant kept in the shade.

Name_____

Our Solar System

Here are the names of all the planets in our solar system. But they are all scrambled! Unscramble each planet name and write it on the line.

1. RCRYUME _____

2. SEVUN _____

3. THARE _____

4. RAMS _____

5. PREJUIT _____

6. NASTUR _____

7. SURANU _____

8. PENNUTE _____

9. LOUPT _____

© Harcourt

Name_____

Let the Sun Shine In

Most people say that they feel happier on a sunny day. They have more energy and the whole world looks brighter. How about you? Keep a diary for a week. Each day, record the weather. Then write a sentence about your mood. Compare your diary with those of your classmates.

Monday Weather _____

Mood _____

Tuesday Weather _____

Mood _____

Wednesday Weather _____

Mood _____

Thursday Weather _____

Mood _____

Friday Weather _____

Mood _____

Saturday Weather _____

Mood _____

Sunday Weather _____

Mood _____

Maps Old and New

BACKGROUND

Summary

Did you ever wish you could get a bird's-eye view of your neighborhood, your state, or the whole country? You can—on a map! Maps show you what a place looks like from the air. Maps point out streets, airports, highways, farms, and rivers. Some show the depths of oceans, while others display topography, the physical features of the land.

There are many kind of maps, and each one has a special purpose. A political map shows the boundaries between counties, states, and countries. A road map shows you how to get from one place to another. A weather map contains temperatures, cold or warm fronts, and an answer to a frequently asked question: What's it like outside?

Maps have their own special language, too. To read a map, you have to know what certain symbols mean. Most maps have a key, or legend, which is a guide to that map's symbols. People have been using maps for centuries. At first, they were made on clay or animal skins. As the world changes, maps change, too.

FAST FACTS

■ A map is like an aerial photograph of an area.

■ A map symbol represents a feature or object on the ground.

■ A legend explains what features or objects the symbols represent.

■ A mapmaker is called a cartographer.

■ The earliest maps were made in about 6,200 B.C.

READING TIPS

Before Reading

■ Discuss some tips for map reading. The key tells you what the little pictures or symbols on the map mean. For example, an airplane may stand for an airport, a thick blue line may stand for a large highway, and a thinner dashed line may stand for a country road. Maps also have a compass rose that shows you the major directions: north, south, east and west. Maps also point out distance. The distance on a map is much shorter than the distance in the "real world" because a whole town, state, or country is shown on a piece of paper. The scale tells how to estimate how far one place is from another. For example, every inch on the map may stand for a distance of 10 miles. Many maps also have a grid. The map is ruled into boxes, and the letters and numbers on the sides help you locate an area.

■ Maps need to be detailed enough so that you can actually find where you're going! There are all kinds of maps. For example, sailors use a special kind of map, called a chart, which shows coastlines and water depths; some people use an atlas when they need to see whole countries together in small scale. Large-scale maps are used for local areas, when you need to see details in a city or neighborhood.

■ Show children some different maps so they get a better sense of what you mean: show maps of your town, as well as of the United States and of the world. Point out where your town is on a United States map. Point out other places, such as Washington, D.C.; New York; Los Angeles.

Critical Thinking

■ Ask children if their family has ever been on a car trip. Did they use a map?

■ Discuss how far some children may have traveled. Is it far to their friend's house? What is the distance to Florida? A grandparents' house?

■ Are there other ways people can figure out where they are going? Discuss how landmarks can help people remember locations. For example, when going to Sydney's house you have to turn left at the blinking yellow light; or, to get to Adam's house, look for a big ice cream store on the corner.

■ Look at a map of Earth. Explain what the equator is (an imaginary line around the middle of Earth and point out the division between the Northern and Southern Hemispheres). What countries are in the Eastern Hemisphere? (Africa, Asia, Australia)

Activities

■ Draw a map of your town. How far is your house from school?

■ Early explorers set out to find new worlds without the help of maps. Many believed the world was flat. If you were exploring, what kind of new world would you like to find?

EXTENSION ACTIVITIES

LOOKING AT PHOTOGRAPHS

Why is reading a map important?

A UNITED STATES ADVENTURE

Skills: Cognitive Thinking, Current Events
Curriculum Area: Language Arts

Cut out photos of various cities in the United States Alternatively, encourage children to bring in their own pictures from vacations they've taken (and places they've been). Have each child choose one location and then create a report about it. Have them point it out on a map. Encourage creativity. For example, have children pretend to be travel agents promoting that place. Have children use the copying master "Take a Trip!" to create a brochure.

MAP RACE

Skills: Reading, Mapping Skills
Curriculum Area: Social Studies

Take a careful look at a large map in your classroom. It should have symbols, labels, and a legend on it. With the class, make a list of the different symbols, town names, parks, natural landmarks, and other kinds of information the map shows. Put each item on your list on a separate index card, and place all the cards in a hat or paper bag. Mount the large map in a place all students can see. Then divide the class into two teams. Pull a card from the bag and read aloud what it says. One child from each team should locate the item on the map. The team that identifies the most items wins.

ANSWER KEY

READER

Think and Respond 1. When borders or country names change, maps change; also, new technology like satellites helps us make different kinds of maps. 2. Old maps of the United States do not show all of the 50 states. 3. Possible responses: You may need a map when you take a car trip, when you go on a hike, when you visit a zoo, or when you study geography.

Make a Map Children's maps should be fairly accurate representations of the classroom. The maps should include labels for all objects that are shown.

Take a Trip!

Where would you like to visit? Find out all about it. Take notes here. Then create a travel brochure for the place on a separate sheet of paper.

Where do you want to go? _____

How far is it from your home? _____

How will you get there? _____

What is the weather like there? _____

What landmarks will you see there?

_____

What will you do for fun there?

_____

Why do you think this is a good place for a vacation?

_____

_____

Draw a picture of your destination.

Name_____

How Far?
How Long?

How long does it take you to get to school? That depends how close together your home and your school are. Think about time and distance by answering the questions below.

It takes me _____ minutes to get to school.
My school is far from/near home.

I can get to the movies in _____ minutes if Mom drives me. If I walk it would take _____ minutes.

When I mail a letter, I walk _____ minutes to the post office.

The best pizza place is _____ minutes from my house.

I like to ride my bike to the library. It takes me _____ minutes to get there from home, and it takes _____ minutes to get there from school.

Himalayan Mountains

BACKGROUND

Summary

The people of Nepal call it Sagarmatha or "goddess of the sky." Those in Tibet use the word Chomolungma, "mother goddess of the universe." In any language, the Himalayan mountain range, in southern Asia, astonishes with its scope and size. This vast range earned another nickname from its many visitors: they call it "the place where Earth meets Sky." Its star attraction is Mt. Everest, the tallest mountain in the world. Many people come from all over the world to climb it. Some have been successful; many have not. The word *Himalaya* actually comes from a Sanskrit phrase meaning "Abode of Snow." Indeed, these mountains are icy cold and snow-capped. They are also gorgeous. The mountains have a huge influence on the people living here. Their sheer beauty attracts visitors, their height attracts adventurers, and their vastness invites readers to learn all they can.

FAST FACTS

■ *Himalaya* is a Sanskrit word that literally means abode of snow, from hima, "snow," and alaya, "abode." The ancient pilgrims of India who traveled in these mountains named them.

■ The first person to climb to the top of Mt. Everest was Sir Edmund Hillary, on May 29, 1953.

■ The first woman to reach the top was Junko Tabei of Japan, on May 16, 1975.

■ Mt. Everest rises 29,028 feet (8,848 m) above sea level. It is located on the border of Nepal and China.

■ No plant life grows near the mountain's top due to powerful winds, cold temperatures, and little oxygen.

■ The oldest man to climb Mt. Everest was Lev Sarkisov from the Republic of Georgia, in 1999. He was 60 years old.

■ In 1998, the greatest number of climbers to date (73) ascended Mt. Everest. Just two years earlier, 15 climbers had died trying to make the trek to the top.

READING TIPS

Before Reading

■ Point out the Himalayas on a map to show their vastness. The Himalayas extend from west to east for about 1,550 miles (2,494 meters) and pass through both India and Tibet. The range is divided into the Western Himalayas, the Central Himalayas, and the Eastern Himalayas.

■ Politics dictates where visitors can travel. Because the mountain range lies close to sensitive international border regions, there are disputes over which part belongs to which country. Special permission is often required to visit certain areas near the borders.

■ The Himalayas, like other parts of the world where people intervene, is considered a fragile ecosystem. Because so many people want to visit, there is a new infrastructure of roads built into the mountains. To build roads, dynamite blasted through rocks and created a danger of landslides. Debris left by climbers and overgrazing by their pack animals cause other environmental problems.

■ Discuss the kinds of people that live here. Look at the pictures in your book for clues. They live a simple life. The ones that work to guide others up the mountains are called sherpas.

Critical Thinking

■ Discuss what life would be like in the shadows of these great mountains. Some people find religious tranquility and pray in beautiful temples located along the mountain route. To them, the magnitude of this range is a powerful force of nature that has spiritual meaning.

■ Climbing Mt. Everest is extremely difficult. Can children think why? (The weather is brutal, cold and snowy, with powerful winds; the low oxygen levels at high altitudes can cause brain damage.)

Activities

■ Have you visited any mountains? How about the top of a skyscraper? Brainstorm a list of high places with children. Have them find out the altitudes of these sites and compare them. What's the highest place they found? How does the Sears Tower compare with Mt. Everest?

EXTENSION ACTIVITIES

LOOKING AT PHOTOGRAPHS:

Would you want to climb these mountains?

TALK ABOUT CLIMATE

Skills: Observation, Cognitive Thinking
Curriculum Areas: Geography, Social Studies
Climate is not the same as weather; weather can change within minutes, but climate describes a region's weather conditions over a long period of time. The climate of a region can affect its landscape and life. Spend a week documenting the weather in your area. Give children a chart with the days of the week, and have them draw pictures and describe the weather each day. Is there a force of nature in your area, such as a large mountain, an ocean or a lake that affects your weather? Discuss.

PASSPORT TO INDIA

Skills: Current Events, Research
Curriculum Area: Social Studies
Use your imagination to journey to India. Talk about the sights and sounds there—including elephants in the streets! India's culture is diverse, the result of its own traditions combined with years of outside influences. Today, more than 1 billion people live in a nation that is about one-third the size of

the United States—but ten times more crowded! It is the world's largest democracy, though it is difficult to govern. Indians speak more than 800 languages. Hindi is the national language, but many people still resist speaking it. They want to speak their own dialect. Discuss the caste system, which began around 1500 B.C. when powerful warriors imposed their social structure on the Himalayan people. Castes were unchanging groups; each group had to live, eat, get married, and die within their own caste. People were not allowed to mix. At the top of the caste system were the Brahmins—the priests, teachers and judges. Next came the warriors, called Kshatriya; farmers and merchants formed the Vaisay, and the Sudras were laborers. Ask: Does this system sound fair?

ANSWER KEY

COPYING MASTER

Page 36 Statement 3 is the only false answer.

READER

Think and Respond 1. They are the highest mountains in the world. **2.** Himalayan people make wool and act as sherpas to earn money. **3.** Possible responses: I would like to visit the Himalayas because it looks very beautiful and very different from where I live; I am curious about the animals and people there.

Write a Letter Children's letters should include information about themselves, such as what their home and school lives are like.

HIMALAYAN MOUNTAINS

An Imaginary Trip

You're going to the Himalayas—at least in your imagination. Where would you like to visit, and why? Write a list of what you'd like to see and do during your trip. This list is called an agenda.

Places I'd Like to Visit in the Himalayas

_____

_____

Animals I Would Like to See

_____

_____

People I Would Like to Meet

_____

_____

What I Would Bring Back as a Souvenir

_____

_____

Which One Is Not True?

The following statements are all true except ONE. Which one is it? Circle it.

1. The Himalayan Mountains are the highest in the world.

2. People have died trying to climb Mt. Everest.

3. The people that live here only have one religion.

4. People come from all over the world to climb Mt. Everest.

5. The Himalayans are a fragile ecosystem.

Pueblo Storyteller Dolls

BACKGROUND

Summary

How many times have you heard "Once upon a time"? Sharing stories—whether it's reading a book before bedtime or telling a tall tale around a campfire—gives the teller and listener time together to imagine, listen, and learn. Storytelling is an ancient art. From the paintings on walls of Egyptian tombs that told stories of daily life, to the folktales of Africa that warned generations of listeners about the tricksters among us, stories link us together and to the past. The Bible itself puts into print stories that parents passed on to their children for generations before paper even existed!

For the Pueblos, a Native American people, the storytelling process has special meaning. Their traditional tales convey to children the history, culture, geography, and language of the Pueblos. But what's really unique is the way they share their heritage. Human storytellers use ceramic dolls as their narrators! Made from the clay of their land and dyes from native plants, these ceramic "Pueblo storytellers" look like parents or grandparents. Clay children crowd their laps, looking captivated by the story. The Pueblos believe that by passing on their folklore, they are also presenting imaginative ways to help their listeners solve problems, make better decisions, and take wiser actions. Pueblo storytelling passes on the wisdom of their culture.

FAST FACTS

■ Storyteller figurines range in height from approximately 2 inches to 10 inches.

■ Thousands of Native American Pueblo people live in New Mexico. Each pueblo has its own government, as well as its own ceremonies and rituals. Many also have their own dialect, or language.

■ In 1960, Taos Pueblo, near Santa Fe, New Mexico, was designated a National Historic Landmark.

■ Taos Pueblo in New Mexico is the largest surviving multi-storied Pueblo structure in the United States.

■ Many centuries before European explorers found their way to the Western Hemisphere, the Pueblo Indians developed their own distinctive civilization.

■ The Pueblo Indians are a peace-loving people; their lives are lived in harmony with the environment and with each other.

■ Nearly all Pueblo populations are divided into clans. Clan members take turns in the Pueblo government and in assuming responsibility for traditional tribal ceremonies.

■ The Pueblo Indians still retain their ancient ceremonies and customs.

READING TIPS

Before Reading

■ Discuss storytelling as an ancient art. To be a storyteller, you need is a vivid imagination and a clear voice to tell the tale, using emotion as you speak. A good storyteller captures the audience's attention and knows when to use silence as part of the story.

■ Talk about how important it is to be a good listener.

■ Talk about what *pueblo* means (a town or village). It can also mean "a communal dwelling" or, when it begins with a capital P, it can refer to a member of a group of Indian peoples living in pueblo villages in New Mexico and Arizona since prehistoric times.

Critical Thinking

■ The Pueblo storyteller dolls are considered folk art, a craft based on traditional stories and folklore. The dolls are something that are part of the Native American culture and have been passed down from generation to generation. Can you think of other works of art that are considered folk art? How about a handcrafted banjo from the Kentucky Hills? A quilt from colonial times?

■ Ask: If you were a storyteller, what kinds of stories would you want to tell? Would you like to tell outer-space stories, futuristic stories, or stories that deal with the past? Discuss with children the kinds of stories that most appeal to them. Talk about the kinds of stories that exist, such as western, mystery, ghost story, science fiction, autobiography, and fiction, and explain the differences.

■ Discuss: Why is it important to pass down stories? Does your family share stories from the past? What kinds of stories would you tell your children?

Activities

■ Pass a simple object, such as a stone, a mug, or a notebook. Each child must say one word describing the object without repeating what has been said. See how many times the object can go around the classroom before you run out of things to say. Children should not feel compelled to use only adjectives; you can also say any words that they associate with the object, such as "homework" for a notebook or "coffee" for a mug.

■ Ask: If you were collecting family stories, what are some questions you'd ask? (Where were you born? How many people were in your family? What did your house look like? Who were some of your best friends? etc.) Talk about the importance of making sure a story tells *how, where, why, what* and *who*.

■ Ask: What questions would you ask a Pueblo storyteller?

EXTENSION ACTIVITIES

LOOKING AT PHOTOGRAPHS:

Why do you think the Pueblos use dolls to tell stories?

READING RAINBOW
Skill: Listening
Curriculum Area: Language Arts
Start a storytelling session. Plan it at a certain time each day for a week. You can use a story-starter, such as "One day, I got up in the morning, and...." Have children sit in a circle and "pass" the story by adding their ideas. Stop the storytelling at a critical point in the session, so the children will be eager to continue the next day.

LOCAL HISTORY
Skills: Reporting, Current Events
Curriculum Area: Social Studies
Just as the Pueblo Indians use stories to keep alive the history of their culture, so too should children know about the history of where they live. As a project, go the local historical society or library to get information about how your school's city or town got its name. Alternatively, they could find out how some of the busiest streets were named, perhaps even the street where your school is located. Are there any interesting stories about the town? Any places that are famous? Discuss as a class.

ANSWER KEY

READER

Think and Respond 1. Storyteller dolls may look like people or like animals. **2.** Storytelling is important to Pueblos because children learn about their heritage through the stories. **3.** Possible responses: It's the only way to make sure everyone knows family history; it brings families together; then children can make sure to tell the stories to their children.

Make a Doll Before making the doll from available materials, children should decide what it will look like. Children's stories should be creative, telling something about the doll.

© Harcourt

All About Me

Before you write a story, you need to know your characters. Answer the questions. Then write a story—about you!

My name is _____ .

My hair color is _____ .

My eyes are _____ .

For fun, I like to _____

_____ .

I have _____ people in my family.

I am _____ years old.

A surprising fact about me is _____

_____

_____ .

Tell Your Own Tale!

Create the beginnings of a tale by filling in the blanks below. Then, draw a picture to go with your tale.

One morning I woke up and _____.
I couldn't believe my eyes! So I went downstairs, and
told my brother all about it. I said, " _____
_____."
At first he just looked at me. Then he laughed and said,
" _____
_____
_____. Let's go have some breakfast."
So we walked into the kitchen, and there on the kitchen
counter, we saw_____
_____
_____!
"See! I told you!" I said to my brother. "Now what do
you have to say?" My brother just grinned and answered,
" _____
_____."

Ellis Island

BACKGROUND

Summary

America is a nation of immigrants. Many of us have roots that go back to other countries— countries in Europe, Africa, the Caribbean or Asia. Millions sailed into New York Harbor, saw the Statue of Liberty, and passed through Ellis Island, which was the great immigration station located in Upper New York Bay. Situated southwest of Manhattan, Ellis Island first served as an arsenal and a fort. However, from 1892 through 1954, it became a bustling port of entry into the United States. So many people came to Ellis Island from other countries in search of freedom and economic opportunity that historians created a term for this massive immigration: a wave. The first wave of immigration came from northern Europe (Ireland, England, Germany and Scandina-vian countries) because of the upheaval brought on by the Industrial Revolution. A second wave streamed out of southern and eastern Europe from 1890 to 1924. Many of these people were fleeing high taxes, poverty, overpopulation, oppression, and religious persecution. They all saw America as a land of fortune and promise. Ellis Island is now a museum, part of the Statue of Liberty National Monument, and is open to tourists year-round.

READING TIPS

Before Reading

■ Talk about children's backgrounds. Ask: Where did your great-grandparents come from? Point out some of those countries on a map. Talk about your own family's roots.

■ Discuss how widespread immigration was. Over 100 million Americans can trace their ancestry to someone who passed through Ellis Island.

■ Walk children through the process. Discuss how each person that stepped off a steamship was scrutinized for disease or disability. Sometimes that meant an immigrant's staying for days in the infirmary; other times it meant being shipped back to his or her native country. Talk about how noisy and crowded it was at the immigration office. Imagine thousands of people at one time speaking a variety of languages. Sometimes officials taking immigrants' names couldn't understand them so they shortened or simplified them on the records. For example, Rosenstadsten could become Rosen.

■ Once people were processed, they descended from the Registry Room down the "Stairs of Separation," called this because they marked the parting of ways for many family and friends with different destinations. Some went to railroad ticket offices and trains headed north, south, east, or west.

FAST FACTS

■ Ellis Island was the chief immigration station for the United States between 1892 and 1954.

■ It is estimated that 40 percent of all Americans has an ancestor who arrived at Ellis Island.

■ More than 12 million immigrants passed through Ellis Island between 1892 and 1954.

■ Ellis Island is named in honor of its original owner, Samuel Ellis.

■ On average, 5,000 people a day were processed through the immigration office at Ellis Island.

■ It took about five hours for one person to pass through the inspection process.

■ Ellis Island is one of the most famous landmarks in the world.

■ After a six-year, $162 million renovation, Ellis Island reopened to the public as a museum in 1990.

Critical Thinking

■ Ask: Do you think it was scary passing through Ellis Island? Children were asked their name to make sure they weren't deaf or unable to speak, and those that looked over the age of two were taken from their mothers' arms and made to walk.

■ Discuss the wide range of emotions people must have felt. They had no idea what the future held for them; they had given up their old world for a new one. They had to pass health tests, answer a series of questions, and deal with government bureaucracy before ever stepping onto American soil.

■ Ask: Do you think women and children were treated fairly? Unescorted women and children were detained until their safety was assured through the arrival of a telegram, letter or prepaid ticket from a waiting relative. Ask: How would you have felt being examined that way?

Activities

■ Make a family tree. Start with yourself, and then add your parents. Where were your parents born? Now write the names of your grandparents. Where were they born? Go back as far as your family members can remember. Genealogy is the study of your family's lineage.

■ Pretend you used a time machine. It's 1915 and you and your family have entered into Ellis Island's great Registry Room. Reread the book and look at the photographs. Now write some of your impressions. What do you see in the Registry Room? What can you hear? How much luggage do you have with you? How do you feel? What does the room smell like? Are you hungry? Are you scared? Write down at least three observations or emotions.

■ Immigrants coming to this country had to learn a new language and adapt to new customs. Have children think about customs that are unique to their school or community. Discuss what it would be like for a newcomer learning about these customs for the first time.

EXTENSION ACTIVITIES

LOOKING AT PHOTOGRAPHS
What surprises you most about Ellis Island?

BUILD VOCABULARY
Skill: Vocabulary
Curriculum Area: Language Arts
Define *genealogy* (the study of family descent or lineage); *ancestor* (a family member from whom a person is descended); and *immigrant* (a person who comes to live permanently in one country from another country). Talk to children about their personal experiences with these terms.

IMMIGRANT EXPERIENCE
Skills: Creative Thinking, Empathy, Current Events
Curriculum Area: Social Studies
Imagine that a new child is joining your class tomorrow. This new situation is not unlike that of an immigrant coming to this country for the first time. What can you do to help the person adapt to your classroom and your school? Discuss as a class how you can make him/her more comfortable.

ANSWER KEY

READER
Think and Respond 1. Ellis Island was once used as an immigration station. **2.** There was a lot of noise at Ellis Island because so many people arrived there. **3.** Possible responses: I hope that my family is waiting for me; I am so glad to be here; I am scared because I don't know much English.

Interview a Partner Children's interviews should reflect the thoughts and feelings of someone seeing the Statue of Liberty for the first time and the experience of entering Ellis Island.

© Harcourt

Pack It Up!

Immigrants coming to America could pack only a few precious things. They were not able to bring lots of baggage. What items would you pack if you were going to start a new life in a new land?

Clothing _____

_____

_____

Books or Toys _____

_____

_____

Photographs _____

_____

_____

Other Precious Items _____

_____

_____

My Trip Journal

TIME FOR KIDS READERS
COPYING MASTER

Some people who arrived at Ellis Island kept a journal of their trip. In it, they wrote about what they saw, who they met and how it felt to be where they were.
Write about a trip you took.

Where did you go? _____

Who went with you? _____

How did you get there? _____

What did you see? _____

Did you meet anyone? _____

What was the best part of the trip? the worst?

_____

_____

How did you feel about going there, being there, and returning home?

_____

_____

World Landmarks

BACKGROUND

Summary

Imagine being so famous that millions of people come to see you every day. They take pictures. They gawk. They look up at you—sometimes *way* up. Then they go home and tell their friends, "I saw a famous landmark." You may have already heard of, or even seen some of the world's most famous landmarks. Some include the Golden Gate Bridge in San Francisco, California; the Leaning Tower of Pisa in Italy; the Taj Mahal in India; Stonehenge in England; and the Colosseum in Rome. They are one-of-a-kind structures, which is what makes them so special and treasured.

Landmarks can be natural or humanmade. Pikes Peak in Colorado and Old Man of the Mountain in New Hampshire stand tall as two natural landmarks. Humanmade landmarks often become symbols of their cities, such as San Francisco's Golden Gate Bridge and the Eiffel Tower in Paris. The word *landmark* is also used as an adjective. For example, a building or a national park can be given "landmark status," meaning it is recognized as historically important, and so has laws to protect it from being altered or damaged.

One national landmark that stands as a symbol of the freedom that the United States offers to its many immigrants actually came from another country. It was a gift from the government of France to the United States. The Statue of Liberty stands in New York harbor. It stands 111 feet (33.9 m) tall from the heel of her foot to the top of her head, and her index finger measures 8 feet (2.4 m). When the Statue of Liberty was constructed, it cost a total of $700,000. Of this amount, French citizens donated about $400,000 for the statue, and Americans donated another $300,000 for the pedestal and for erecting the statue. Compare this with the cost of repairing the statue in 1986: it cost the United States approximately $30 million!

FAST FACTS

■ The Golden Gate Bridge is not golden at all; it is red.

■ The Golden Gate Bridge has been heralded as one of the top construction achievements of the twenieth century.

■ It is estimated that 9 million people from around the world visit the Golden Gate Bridge each year.

■ Construction began on the Leaning Tower of Pisa in 1173 and continued, with two long interruptions, for about two hundred years.

■ The Leaning Tower of Pisa was not designed to lean; it was meant to be vertical; it started to lean during its construction.

■ The Taj Mahal, renowned for its architectural magnificence and beauty, is synonymous with India.

■ Machu Picchu means "manly peak." Its ruins feature terraced stonework and 3,000 steps!

■ Machu Picchu was most likely a royal estate and religious retreat. It was built around A.D. 1460.

■ About 1,200 people lived in Machu Picchu, most of them women, children, and priests. The buildings are thought to have been planned under the supervision of Inca architects.

■ Machu Picchu was discovered in 1911 by a Yale University professor, Hiram Bibghan.

READING TIPS

Before Reading

■ Have children talk about the word *landmark*. What does it mean to them? Can they name landmarks in their city or state?

A landmark has various elements that make it unique. The Golden Gate Bridge, for example, has tremendous towers, sweeping cables, and a large span. Find San Francisco on a map. Also point out Pisa, Italy; and the locations of the Taj Mahal (Agra, India) and Machu Picchu. (near Cuzco, Peru)

Discuss what an architect does. (designs and plans buildings) Every building, including your home, had an architect involved in planning it.

Critical Thinking

Talk about how Washington, D.C., is a city full of landmarks. Discuss the White House, the Capitol, and the Smithsonian Museums. What makes a landmark special?

Ask: If you were architects, what kind of building would you like to make?

Ask: Why are landmarks important?

Reread the book. Are there any similarities between the landmarks listed? Any differences?

Activities

When separated, *landmark* is really *land* and *mark*: a compound word. Think of other words that begin with land but end with another word. Work together as a class to make a list. (Possible responses: landowner, landholder, landfill, landfall, landmass, landlord, landlocked, landform, landslide)

Many landmarks have inspired artists to draw them. Review the photos in your book. Which ones inspire you? Draw one of them. Write a sentence underneath explaining why you like it.

EXTENSION ACTIVITIES

LOOKING AT PHOTOGRAPHS

What makes the Golden Gate Bridge a landmark?

THERE'S NO PLACE LIKE HOME

Skills: Mapreading, Sorting and Classifying
Curriculum Area: Language Arts

Investigate the landmarks of your state by exploring the website created by the Library of Congress. Select "Explore the States," and then choose your state or neighboring states and see what you can discover about nearby landmarks, both natural and humanmade.

WISH YOU WERE HERE: A LANDMARKS ALBUM

Skills: Observation, Critical Thinking, Current Events
Curriculum Area: Social Studies

Taking photos of famous landmarks is a good way to remember them and to record your visit. Have children take photos (or draw pictures) of their favorite local landmark. (It can be their house, their favorite playground, or a statue.) Use the copying master "Design a Landmark" as a starting point. Have children mount their photos on paper and add captions that explain what makes each one special. Bind them together into a "Landmarks Album," and add this book to your classroom library. Alternatively, have children share their photos with members of another class and answer those children's questions about the landmarks they chose.

ANSWER KEY

COPYING MASTER

Page 47 Machu Picchu, Peru; Leaning Tower of Pisa, Italy; Golden Gate Bridge, United States; Eiffel Tower, France; Taj Mahal, India.

READER

Think and Respond 1. A landmark is something that makes you think of a certain place. **2.** A mountain, such as Mt. Kilimanjaro, is one landmark not built by people. **3.** Possible responses: the Empire State Building, the Eiffel Tower, Mt. Rainier.

Draw a Landmark Children's drawings should show a landmark found in their neighborhood.

Name_____

Where in the World?

Looking at landmarks can take you around the world! Reread the book, and see if you can match each landmark with its country.

Machu Picchu   India

Leaning Tower of Pisa   United States

Golden Gate Bridge   Peru

Eiffel Tower   Italy

Taj Mahal   France

Name_____

Design a Landmark!

Landmarks can be buildings, monuments, or sculptures. Humanmade landmarks often honor an event or a person. If you could create a monument, what or whom would you honor? Draw it below, and explain what your landmark is all about.

_____

_____

_____

_____

© Harcourt

Historic St. Augustine

BACKGROUND

Summary

Spanish explorer Juan Ponce de León believed in miracles. He also had faith that he would experience one himself, if he looked long and hard enough. That quest found Ponce de León cruising the Atlantic in the spring of 1513. Finding a harbor, he sailed in and disembarked in lush tropical gardens whose blooms and ferns made it look like paradise. He thought he'd surely find here the source for the miracle he had heard about: the fountain of youth. Ponce de León named this wonderland *La Florida*, which means "land of flowers," and claimed it for Spain.

About 50 years later, Admiral Don Pedro Menéndez de Avilés arrived to colonize the territory and drive out any pirates or settlers. He arrived in Florida on August 28, 1565, the feast day of St. Augustine. When he and his soldiers took over, he renamed the village to honor that saint. This small city was founded 55 years before the Pilgrims landed on Plymouth Rock, making it the oldest permanent European settlement in North America. Today we know it as St. Augustine.

What does a really old city look like? St. Augustine, not far from Jacksonville, provides a window into precolonial life. Here you'll see America's oldest schoolhouse, built in 1763, as well as the two-room houses typical of the time. You can even participate in daily living activities from pre-European times in the hands-on Old Florida Museum, try writing with a quill pen, or draw water from a pitcher pump.

FAST FACTS

■ In 1819 Spain ceded Florida to the U.S.; Florida became a U.S. territory in 1821.

■ Florida became the 27th state admitted to the Union in 1845.

■ In addition to its vast history, St. Augustine has forty-three miles of enjoyable beaches.

■ St. Augustine has been careful to preserve its buildings, making it a top destination spot and a center of colonial Spanish culture.

■ St. Augustine is the site of an important Indian burial ground that dates back to prehistoric times.

READING TIPS

Before Reading

■ St. Augustine is located on Florida's east coast. Point out its location on a map. (near Jacksonville)

■ Ponce de León was really searching for the Fountain of Youth when he happened upon St. Augustine. The Spring House is the spot where he drank water, hoping for eternal youth. Today you can see the stone cross in the ground, still in its original place, preserved along with the spring in a building that includes a diorama depicting the arrival of the Spanish. And yes, visitors can taste the water!

Critical Thinking

■ The Timucua Indians were living on the land Ponce de León claimed for Spain. What do you think happened when these cultures collided? Talk about what it means to adapt to someone's customs and differences. Can people work out their differences in peaceful ways? Discuss.

■ Talk about what it must have been like to find and explore an unknown land. Would it be scary? Exciting? Do you think other people would believe your findings? What could you do to record what you learned and convince others?

■ Ask: Does a fountain of youth really exist? Can drinking water make you younger? Discuss as a class. Talk about some other myths and folktales.

Activities

■ You have just landed on another frontier, not unlike the brave new world Ponce de León discovered. Write a story about your travels.

■ Go on a treasure hunt! Give children a list of clues (for instance, "it is sharp and yellow:" a pencil) and have them look for items in the classroom. Encourage children to observe the room carefully and write down their own clues for "hidden treasure." Have children read their clues and challenge you and classmates to find it.

EXTENSION ACTIVITIES

LOOKING AT PHOTOGRAPHS

How do you know that this is an old city?

FAMILY LIFE

Skills: Observation, Critical Thinking, Current Events
Curriculum Area: Social Studies

Typical family life is shown in the photo of the Gallegos House (page 6). Cooking was done on a *fogon,* a typical Mediterranean stove. In the winter, heat was provided by the *brasero,* a metal pan of hot coals. There was a small garden outside: here, the family would grow herbs and vegetables to eat. There would also be chickens and pigs roaming the yard. Discuss some of the chores children had to do (fetch water, cook, garden, take care of the animals). Ask: What are some of the chores you are responsible for? Are they similar to or different from those of the youngsters of Spanish colonial Florida? Discuss, too, how many young boys were taught woodworking or blacksmithing as a way of learning a trade for their future. Many worked as apprentices (helpers) to their fathers or friends. Many girls, on the other hand, may have learned skills such as

cooking, cleaning, mending clothes and taking care of their younger siblings.

MAKE A TIME CAPSULE

Skills: Creative Thought, Current Events
Curriculum Areas: Social Studies, Language Arts

What was life like in the past? One way children can find out what life was like in the past is to ask an adult relative or friend. Send a note home explaining that the class will create a "time capsule." Ask family members to lend pictures of items from their childhood or to answer the questions on the copying master "In My Life." Each picture must have a very short description and be labeled (in small writing) with the year it was used. Once you've collected pictures and reminiscences, place them in a box. Have children select a picture or read a passage to share with classmates. Then have the reader ask the class: What year was this used? Consider inviting family members to share their memories of childhood.

ANSWER KEY

READER

Think and Respond 1. A living history museum, with restored homes and tour guides, can be found in St. Augustine. **2.** Juan Ponce de León is the Spanish explorer who landed in Florida in 1513. **3.** Possible responses: What kind of food did you eat? What was your typical day?

Compare Today to Long Ago Children should write down at least three interview questions about life before modern electronics. Encourage children to practice with a partner before conducting the actual interview.

My History

St. Augustine is the birthplace of Florida and the beginning of its history. What is your history? Answer each of the questions below.

1. Where were you born? _____

2. What year? _____

3. What date? _____

4. How many people were in your family then?

_____

5. How many people are in your family now?

_____

6. What is one of your earliest memories?

_____

_____

_____

_____

_____

In My Life

What was life like for your parents, aunts, uncles, or grandparents when they were growing up? In what ways was their childhood like yours? Ask these questions of older family members to find out.

Where were you born? _____

_____

What year were you born? _____

How old were you when you started school? _____

What was the name of your first school?

_____

How did you get to school?

_____

Martin Luther King, Jr.

BACKGROUND

Summary

In 1963 a young Baptist minister from Montgomery, Alabama, led 250,000 people in a march on Washington, D.C. Why? He said it best in a powerful speech, made from the steps of the Lincoln Memorial: "I have a dream . . . that my four children will one day live in a nation where they will not be judged by the color of their skin but by the content of their character." This man, Dr. Martin Luther King, Jr., wanted to defeat segregation by peaceful means. He wanted to achieve equality for African Americans—men, women and children—across the nation.

During King's youth, he experienced the hurt of prejudice just as tens of thousands of African Americans did throughout the South. Just because he was African American, he had to sit at the rear of buses.

He couldn't dine at certain restaurants, stay at certain hotels, or even drink at certain water fountains. Some were "For Whites Only." Dr. Martin Luther King, Jr., decided that when he grew up, he'd find a way to change that.

Under his leadership the Civil Rights movement won many victories against segregation laws, which prevented African Americans from voting, from going to schools with whites, and so on. In 1968, just five years after the march on Washington, King was assassinated. But his dream of a country free of racial discrimination lives on. Since his death many civil rights organizations carry on his work. Since 1986, our nation observes Dr. Martin Luther King, Jr., Day on the third Monday of January, close to his actual birthday of January 15th.

FAST FACTS

■ Dr. Martin Luther King, Jr.'s words inspired millions of Americans of all ethnic groups.

■ Dr. Martin Luther King, Jr., carried the civil rights crusade all over the United States in the 1950s and 1960s. In all, he traveled more than 6 million miles and spoke on more than 2,500 occasions. He was arrested more than 20 times and assaulted 4 times.

■ Dr. Martin Luther King, Jr., married Coretta Scott in Marion, Alabama in 1953; they had four children.

■ In 1958, King's first book, "Stride Toward Freedom," was published. It is about the Montgomery bus boycott.

■ King was awarded the Nobel Peace Prize on December 10, 1964.

■ King was assassinated while he was leading a worker's strike in Memphis, Tennessee, in 1968.

■ Americans celebrated Dr. Martin Luther King, Jr., Day for the first time on January 20, 1986.

READING TIPS

Before Reading

■ Martin Luther King, Jr.'s, famous 1963 speech is known as his "I Have a Dream" speech. It made him famous. He said, "I have a dream that one day this nation will rise up and live out the true meaning of its creed: We hold these truths to be self-evident; that all men are created equal." Talk about the word *equality*. Discuss what discrimination means (showing prejudice against); and what prejudice means (an opinion formed before the facts are known).

■ In 1964—1965 racial discrimination was finally outlawed in the United States. Until then, many African Americans remained second-class citizens, especially in the southern states. Laws dictated where they could eat, where they had to ride on a bus, and so on.

■ In 1955 Rosa Parks, an African American seamstress, was arrested for refusing to give up her bus seat to a white person. She has since become a symbol of the Civil Rights movement. In response to her bravery, Rev. King organized a powerful but peaceful protest. For one year, Dr. Martin Luther King, Jr., and his followers persuaded people to boycott every bus in Montgomery, Alabama, until the segregation of bus seats was declared illegal.

Critical Thinking

■ Have King's ideas taken hold? Discuss civil rights today. Are we truly an "equal" country? Are we a peaceful nation? Are people nice to each other? Do they treat each other fairly?

■ Ask: What do you think Dr. King would think of our world today? Discuss, too, what you think he would be doing. Would he still be a minister? Would he be a politician? the first African American President of the U.S.? Brainstorm some scenarios.

Activities

■ Ask children to imagine that they could write a letter to their children about what they hope the world will be like when they grow up. Ask: What are your dreams for the future? Have children write them down.

■ Ask: What does it mean to be a leader like Dr. King? What character traits do you need? Have children write down at least three things that a leader needs to be effective.

EXTENSION ACTIVITIES

LOOKING AT PHOTOGRAPHS

What does this photo tell you about King and his dream?

BEING BRAVE

Skills: Cognitive Thinking, Reading, Writing
Curriculum Area: Social Studies
Dr. Martin Luther King, Jr., was a very brave man. Discuss what it means to be brave. Ask children about a time when they did something brave. Talk about other courageous African Americans, such as

Rosa Parks, who refused to give up her bus seat, and Ruby Bridges, a 6-year-old who walked through screaming crowds to enter a whites-only school in New Orleans in 1960. Have students research other Americans who took risks for their beliefs.

DAYDREAMER

Skill: Cognitive Thinking
Curriculum Areas: Language Arts, Social Studies
Dr. Martin Luther King, Jr., had a dream. He wanted the whole world to live it. Ask students: What do you dream about? If you could change the world, what would you do? Use the copying master "Daydreamer" to write down your ideas and ways to achieve them.

ANSWER KEY

COPYING MASTER

Page 55 1. Atlanta, Ga.; **2.** a church pastor (or minister, or civil rights leader); **3.** peaceful marches; **4.** the "I Have a Dream" speech; **5.** for all people to be treated equally

READER

Think and Respond 1. Martin Luther King, Jr. was a pastor and a leader for equal rights for all people. **2.** He led peaceful marches and protests to earn rights for people of all races. **3.** Dr. King was a great leader because he stood up for what he thought was right and used peaceful means to achieve his goals.

Write about the Future Children should write a paragraph describing what their lives might be like in the future when one of their hopes or dreams comes true.

© Harcourt

Name_____

Remember Dr. King

Answer the following questions.

1. Where was Martin Luther King, Jr., born?

_____

2. What did he grow up to be?

_____

3. What kinds of demonstrations did he lead?

_____

4. What was his famous 1963 speech called?

_____

5. What was his dream?

_____

_____

_____

Name_____

Daydreamer

**Dr. Martin Luther King, Jr., had a dream.
He wanted all races to live in harmony. A
dream is an idea that you believe in strongly.
What is your dream for a better world?
Write an answer to each of these questions.**

What is your dream?

_____

_____

Why do you want it to come true?

_____

_____

Who can help you with your dream?

_____

_____

How will you make your dream come true?

_____

_____

© Harcourt

At the Museum

BACKGROUND

Summary

Why is she smiling? What is she looking at? What do you think she's thinking? Visitors from all nations ask these questions when they see the painting of Mona Lisa by Leonardo da Vinci hanging in one of the world's most famous museums in Paris, France. Known as the Louvre, this museum is, in itself, a work of art.

One of its buildings was once a royal residence, dating back to the sixteenth century. A medieval fortress, the palace of the kings of France, and a museum for the last two centuries, the architecture of the Louvre Palace bears witness to more than 800 years of history.

Established in 1793 by the French Republic, the Louvre Museum, in the company of the Ashmolean Museum (1683), the Dresden Museum (1744) and the Vatican Museum (1784), was one of the first European museums.

Divided into 7 departments, the Louvre collections incorporate works dating from the birth of the great ancient civilizations of Egypt, Greece and Rome, right up to the first half of the nineteenth century, thereby confirming it as one of the world's great collections.

Today, the Louvre is a vast complex of buildings and courtyards. Glass pyramids, designed by modernist architect I.M.Pei, create a striking entrance in front of the museum's original, classical buildings. To help visitors find their way, the museum's wings are color-coded. Still, you will need a map of the Louvre to find your way and decide what you want to see first.

FAST FACTS

■ The Louvre is one of the world's most famous art galleries.

■ The Louvre houses more than 6,000 European paintings dating from the end of the thirteenth century to the mid-nineteenth century in a wide variety of genres and formats.

■ The Louvre was established in 1793, making it one of the first European museums.

■ The Louvre is forever renovating and restoring its buildings. There is even a shopping area underneath the museum called the Carrousel du Louvre, as well as a continuous garden area that connects it to the famous Jardin des Tuileries.

■ The Louvre is free for people up to the age of 18.

■ Built by Philippe Auguste in 1204, the Louvre originally served as King Charles V's royal chateau.

■ Glass pyramids designed by famous architect I.M. Pei were added to the museum in 1989.

■ The glass pyramids that form the new entrance to the Louvre were controversial and much disliked when they were unveiled in 1989; today they are a Paris landmark.

READING TIPS

Before Reading

■ Ask children to recall a museum they've visited. What was the most interesting thing they saw? Let them know there are all kinds of museums: ethnic museums, children's museums, wax museums, train museums, historical museums, even museums devoted to dentistry and teeth! Planetariums and zoos are kinds of museums, too.

■ Some of the sections in the Louvre include ancient art from Asia, Islamic nations, Egypt, Greece, Italy, Africa, Oceania and the Americas. Visiting the Louvre lets you travel back in time!

■ "Mona Lisa," a painting by Leonardo da Vinci, hangs in the Louvre. It is known as a masterpiece (something done with great skill).

Critical Thinking

■ Discuss: What makes something good enough to be in a museum? Does it have to be old?

■ Ask: What do you like to see in a museum? crafts? paintings? ancient art? antique toys?

Activities

■ Reading this book let children "virtually" visit the Louvre. Ask: What piece of art did you like best? What most impressed you about this museum?

■ The Louvre is a famous landmark. Ask: What are some other landmarks you know? Have children make a postcard that shows their favorite one (e.g., the Eiffel Tower, the Empire State Building, the Taj Mahal, the Golden Gate Bridge, the St. Louis Gateway Arch), and share it with the class.

EXTENSION ACTIVITIES

LOOKING AT PHOTOGRAPHS

Why is this piece of art in a museum? What do you think makes it special?

BUILD VOCABULARY BY DEFINING ART

Skills: Vocabulary, Observation
Curriculum Area: Language Arts

Art comes in many forms. Discuss some terms associated with art, such as *landscape* (a drawing or painting of a scene in nature); a *seascape* (art that shows the sea and ships); a *cityscape* (a representation of city buildings, streets and people); a *portrait* (a painting or drawing of one or more people); a *still life* (a picture of small objects that don't move, such as a basket of fruit or a vase full of flowers); *abstract art* (a picture created with shapes, colors and textures that make an object look nothing like it does in the real world); and *sculpture* (a three-dimensional form made from clay, stone, metal or another material.) Photography can also be art. A masterpiece is something done with great skill. Have children use a library or the Internet to find examples of some of these terms. Have them record their findings on the student copying master "My Art Journal." Can they find one they would call a masterpiece? What makes it a masterpiece?

DESTINATION: PARIS

Skill: Current Events
Curriculum Area: Geography

Tell children: You're going to Paris to see the Louvre. Lucky you! What else will you see in Paris? Discuss the city in general and some of its highlights—for example, the Eiffel Tower, Notre Dame, Versailles, the Seine River, the Arc de Triomphe, La Madeleine, even Disneyland Paris if you want! Point out Paris on a map. Talk about what Paris is like. Ask: How many hours will it take you to fly there? What time is it there now? What is the weather like? What language do the people speak? What kind of food do they eat? Invite a travel agent to visit the class to talk about how to plan a trip to Paris.

ANSWER KEY

READER

Think and Respond 1. The Louvre Museum is famous because it has a huge collection of art from many periods in history. **2.** You would find paintings, sculptures, furniture, and many other precious objects from cultures around the world and throughout history. **3.** Possible responses: I would show art that I liked; art that reflected my culture; art from my favorite time in history.

Write about Art Children should write a paragraph describing why they like a particular art piece from the Reader.

My Art Journal

Choose a painting that you like. Look closely at it, and learn as much as you can about it. Then answer the questions below.

Who painted the artwork you chose?

_____

What is the title of the painting?

_____

What does the title tell you about the painting?

_____

When did the painter create this work?

_____

How old was the painter when he or she painted this?

_____

What do you like about this painting?

_____

_____

_____

_____

Name_____

Portrait of an Artist

Reread "At the Museum." Choose an artist whose work appears in the Louvre. Answer these questions to create a portrait of the artist—with words!

The name of the artist I chose is _____

_____

He or she lived and worked in the _____ century.

The kind of work this artist does is _____

_____

The name of this artist's most famous work is

_____

I like this artist because

_____

_____

_____

_____

_____

© Harcourt

The Mint

BACKGROUND

Summary

The next time you're about to buy a pack of gum or use a pay phone, look at your money. Where do you think it comes from (besides your pocket)? That jingling spare change— specifically, pennies, nickels, dimes, quarters, half-dollars, and the dollar coin— originates at the United States Mint. Each coin is stamped with a special design, which includes its value and often the year it was manufactured. This stamping process is known as minting.

The United States Mint is located in Washington, D.C., and is part of the United States Treasury Department. Branches in Denver and Philadelphia also make coins; it is in these locations that pennies are produced. Today, to keep the American economy flowing smoothly, the United States Mint also maintains facilities in San Francisco and West Point, and has a bullion depository in Fort Knox, Kentucky.

READING TIPS

Before Reading

■ The first United States coins were copper cents made in Philadelphia in 1792. George Washington appointed the first Director of the Mint—a scientist and Philadelphian named David Rittenhouse. Under Rittenhouse's direction, 11,178 copper cents became the first circulated coins.

■ At the United States Bullion Depository in Fort Knox, Kentucky, which stores the Treasury Department's gold and silver, United States Mint Police stand guard 24 hours a day, seven days a week!

■ Point out Mint locations on a map so students get a sense of how widespread the moneymaking process is. Visit the Mint's website for a virtual tour of the Mint today.

Critical Thinking

■ Discuss the process of making money. Machinery does most of the work, but many people need to be on-site to oversee the process and make sure the coins are the right shape and composition. Would you want to work at a Mint?

■ Ask children to name without looking whose face is on the penny, the nickel, the dime, and the quarter. What is the value of each?

■ Brainstorm as a class why money is important. Ask: What would you do if you didn't have the money for essentials?

FAST FACTS

■ The United States Mint was founded in 1792, in Philadelphia, which was then the U.S. Capitol.

■ The first United States coins were copper cents, produced at the Philadelphia Mint.

■ During the Gold rush and westward expansion of the 1800s, people started minting their own coins because the need for hard currency outpaced the production of the Mint!

■ The number of coins minted today is astounding. Denver and Philadelphia alone produce 65 million to 80 million coins a day.

■ The Washington, D.C., location of the United States Mint does not make pennies.

■ A tiny "D" or "P" near the year, called a mintmark, tells you which location — Denver or Philly — made the coin. Pennies without marks are usually made in Philadelphia; this location has a tradition of never marking their pennies.

■ The United States Mint has more than 2,800 employees. It produces about seven hundred coins per minute!

Activities

■ Tell children: You have $2 in change in your pocket. What can that buy? Make a list. Have children do the math. Discuss the fact that what seems like a lot of money often does not go very far. When your great-grandparents were children, ten cents could buy a movie ticket plus an ice-cream pop!

■ Word alert: There's *mint*, the word related to making money, and *mint*, the breath candy you put in your mouth—two words spelled and pronounced exactly the same, but with different meanings. Think of other words that share these traits, for example, *ear* (the body part) and *ear* (the edible part of a corn plant). What about *ball* (a big dance) and *ball* (the toy you play with)? Brainstorm ideas as a class.

EXTENSION ACTIVITIES

LOOKING AT PHOTOGRAPHS

How can you tell which branch of the United States Mint made this coin?

SAVING STATE QUARTERS

Skills: Vocabulary, Current Events
Curriculum Area: Social Studies

Talk about the new 50 State Quarters™ Program featuring designs representing each state. Ask: Do any of you collect coins? Thousands of children are collecting these unique coins—one commemorative quarter for each state in the Union—and learning more about their country's history and heritage. Begin a class collection! Children can "save" the state illustrations by placing a sheet of paper over each new quarter and making a rubbing with a pencil. Alternatively, you can give children a copy of a United States map and have them color in each state as they collect its quarter. Since a new quarter will be released approximately every ten weeks through 2008, you have a timely way to teach key skills for years to come!

PENNY HARVEST

Skills: Current Events, Cognitive Thinking
Curriculum Areas: Social Studies, Math

Explain to children that one penny doesn't buy you much, but a jarful might add up to quite a sum. Still, lots of people throw pennies on the ground or stick them in a drawer. Ask: Can you think of great ways to use those pennies? Talk about short-term goals and long-term goals. A short-term goal might be to save all week so you can buy a slice of pizza on Friday. A long-term might be to save up for an expensive toy. Another long-term goal might be to save to make a contribution to charity. Discuss community needs and suggest to children that they choose one charity to support. How will they gather funds? Ask families and the school community to donate spare pennies. Place a large jar in your room, and have children create posters and flyers to advertise their penny harvest. Invite children to estimate the total as the jar fills. Then visit the bank and bring back dozens of penny rolls. How much did you harvest? Now, give it away!

ANSWER KEY

COPYING MASTER

Page 63: 1. 61 cents, **2.** 67 cents, **3.** 56 cents, **4.** $1.00

Page 64: 1. 4, **2.** 8, **3.** 1, **4.** 1, **5.** 2 bottles of juice, or 4 apples, or 1 bottle of juice and 2 apples

READER

Think and Respond 1. Like a factory, the Mint employs many people, and it manufactures a product—money. **2.** Coins begin as sheets of metal. Then small circles are stamped out of the metal. Next, words and pictures are stamped on both sides, and finally people inspect the coins. **3.** Coins need to be checked carefully because each one must be perfect.

Design a Coin Children's drawings should show an important landmark or place associated with a historic event that occurred in their town or city.

Name_____

Count Your Change

**Look at each set of coins below.
How much is each set worth? Add them up.
Then write the value.**

1. Two quarters, a dime and
a penny. What is the value?

_____

2. One half-dollar, a nickel,
one dime, and two pennies.
What is the value?

_____

3. One penny, two nickels,
two dimes, and one
quarter. What is the value?

_____

4. Three nickels, one dime,
and three quarters.
What is the value?

_____

Name_____

How Much Is That Doggie in the Window?

You love to shop! A stuffed dog costs $5.00, a bottle of juice costs $1.00, an apple costs 50 cents, and a picture frame costs $3.00. You have $5.00. How many things can you buy?

1. How many bottles of juice can you buy if you also want an apple?

_____

2. How many apples can you buy if you also want a bottle of juice?

_____

3. How many stuffed dogs can you buy?

_____

4. How many picture frames can you buy?

_____

5. If you buy one picture frame, what can you buy with your change? List as many examples as money will buy!

_____

_____

_____

THE MINT

Robert Fulton

BACKGROUND

Summary

Have you ever had an idea that was so good you had to share it with others? Robert Fulton had plenty. At first they were just dreams, but Fulton was determined. He put his ideas into practice, working and tinkering with them until one day, after much trial and error, his plans actually worked.

Fulton was interested in the dynamics and engineering of boats. In 1797 he devised a boat that could stay underwater; it was our first submarine. Later he invented a boat that used steam for power. The first steamboat he tried failed. It sailed up the Seine River in Paris, France, and stalled. When he tried again in New York harbor, jeering crowds taunted him from the docks. But after one false start, the *Clermont* proudly tooted its way up New York's Hudson River in the summer of 1807.

Along the banks of the river people stared and gaped at the strange-looking machine; others ran screaming into the woods. The shrill whistle startled the fishermen at night, and when they saw the boat heading their way, with a column of fire rising from its smokestack, they thought some monster had come to devour them. Their cries and prayers echoed through the darkness, contrasting strangely with the jeers of the city crowds hours before.

FAST FACTS

■ As a young man, Fulton dreamed of becoming a painter and went to Paris to study.

■ Fulton was of Irish descent, and his father, Robert Fulton, Sr., moved the family to Pennsylvania.

■ People called his first boat—an odd-looking, improbable craft—"Fulton's Folly," but Fulton proved them wrong!

■ Fulton's first successful steamboat, the *Clermont*, was tested on the Hudson River, and took 32 hours to get from New York City to Albany. It moved against the river's current at an average of 5 miles per hour.

READING TIPS

Before Reading

■ Ever since our earliest ancestors discovered that wood floats on water, ships and boats have played a major part in history. The first boats helped people cross rivers and streams and carried hunters into shallow water so they could catch food. Later ships carried people across vast oceans to new worlds. Along the way, the technology of boats and ships improved.

■ Fulton's attempts to create a steamboat met with many failures before eventual success. His boat the *Clermont* was tested on the Hudson River. He had shipped a small steam engine from England and constructed a hull similar to that of ocean-going ships. In the hull, he placed the engine, and on each side, a primitive paddlewheel.

■ The stone house where Fulton was born in 1765 is today a museum. Visitors can tour the house to get a glimpse of what life was like in the mid-eighteenth century. The house is in Quarryville, Pennsylvania, about 100 miles west of Philadelphia. An exhibit in the house documents Fulton's life.

Critical Thinking

■ Robert Fulton was a man of many talents. He was an accomplished artist as well as an inventor. Among his most famous artworks are miniature portraits of prominent Philadelphians, including Benjamin Franklin. Ask: Can one person have more than one career?

■ The great power of a submarine lies in its ability to stay hidden, traveling unseen beneath the water. Ask: Where are places you like to hide?

■ Ask: What else did steamships carry besides people? (goods) Discuss why the steamboat was a major invention at the time.

■ Have children imagine life without planes, trains, cars or motor-driven boats. Discuss how people's lives were changed by each of these forms of transportation.

Activities

■ The way we travel has changed a lot since the eighteenth century. Ask: How did people travel from one city to another before cars or trains existed? How could they journey from the United States to Europe before airplanes came to be? Brainstorm as a class some modes of transportation you think will exist in the future. Will there be flying cars? Solar-powered boats? Airplanes that travel even faster than the Concorde?

EXTENSION ACTIVITIES

LOOKING AT PHOTOGRAPHS

Why do you think Robert Fulton is called a man of many talents? (He painted and invented.)

GREAT MISTAKES

Skills: Reading, Research
Curriculum Area: Language Arts

Some of the best and most useful items we have today came about because of an inventor's mistake! Use the book *Mistakes that Worked* or *The Kid Who Invented the Popsicle* to introduce to children some of these examples, or simply share a few: the chocolate-chip cookie, the ice pop, self-stick notes, and many more. Have the class form small groups and investigate each of these great mistakes. Encourage groups to draw a picture of the "mistake," include the year it happened, and write a short paragraph describing it. Use a bulletin board in your classroom or in the hallway to create a "Timeline of Great Mistakes." Ask: Do you see any similarities among the inventors or the inventions?

INTRODUCE INVENTORS

Skills: Historical Perspective, Cognitive Thinking
Curriculum Area: Social Studies

Introduce other well-known inventors to children. Discuss how important the power of imagination is. Without it, many ideas may not have taken hold. Talk about Margaret Knight (the paper bag); Thomas Edison (the lightbulb); the Wright brothers (the first powered airplane); Garrett Morgan (the traffic signal); Alexander Graham Bell (the telephone); Henry Ford (the car) and Bill Gates (leader in computer revolution). What everyday items do children take for granted, without thinking about their beginning? (For example, electronic games, the microwave, the VCR, the television, the cell phone or beeper, cars) Lead a class discussion about technology. Ask: Does technology change the world? Is that good or bad?

ANSWER KEY

READER

Think and Respond 1. Robert Fulton was known as a painter and as the inventor of the steamboat. **2.** Fulton's idea for the submarine helped later inventors; the steamboat helped people and goods travel to new places. **3.** Possible responses: What else would you like to invent? Do you have advice for young inventors?.

Draw an Invention Children's drawings should show the new inventions they designed. Children should write about why the inventions are important and why people would need them.

Practice Makes Perfect

Robert Fulton had to work on his inventions for a long time until they worked. Sometimes you need to practice many times before you get something right. What kinds of skills do you have to practice so that you get them just right? List them here.

_____

_____

_____

_____

_____

_____

_____

_____

_____

_____

An Inventor's Life

Who invented the pencil you hold in your hand? The traffic light at the corner? Your teddy bear? Choose an item you use every day. Use the library or the Internet to find out who invented it. Write about that person and invention here.

TIME
FOR KIDS
READERS
COPYING MASTER

Did you know that_____ invented

_____?

Here is how that inventor did it:

_____

_____

_____

_____

_____

_____

_____

© Harcourt

ROBERT FULTON

Goods Around the World

BACKGROUND

Summary

Somewhere right now in China, workers may be harvesting rice...the same rice that you will have for dinner six months from now. Perhaps your next favorite sweater is being made in Italy. And did you know that if you turned on a television in Kenya you might see an American sitcom? How did all of these goods—products that we use—get from one place to another?

Many of America's goods come from other countries. They are imported; we receive them from someplace else for the purpose of selling them to American consumers, people who wish to buy them. We get gas at a gas station, and bananas and rice cakes at the supermarket, but in reality the oil may have come from Saudi Arabia, the bananas from Brazil, and the rice in the rice cakes from China.

Why do we import goods from other countries? We may lack the natural resources to produce enough of a given good. Oil is a good example. Some goods, like fruits and vegetables, grow in the United States for only a single season. Importing allows us to eat a nectarine in mid-winter—because it's flown in from Chile where summer is in full swing! The United States also produces many items that we export, or send for sale elsewhere. Iowa corn, Idaho potatoes, and Maine lobsters—not to mention jeans and designer fashions—are in demand all over the world.

FAST FACTS

■ Chinese records of rice cultivation go back 4,000 years.

■ In several Asian languages, the words for rice and food are identical.

■ It has been estimated that half the world's population subsists wholly or partially on rice.

■ Gasoline intended for use in engines is rated by its octane number, an index of quality that reflects its ability to burn evenly.

■ There are five blends of gasoline marketed in the U.S.; since 1992 gasoline has been formulated to evaporate more slowly in hot weather to cut down on smog.

■ In many parts of the world, people keep goats or sheep for their milk which is then made into cheese and yogurt.

■ During the eighteenth century, an agricultural revolution took hold, improving the lives of farmers through the use of fertilizer and the introduction of new crops and breeds of livestock.

■ Sheep shearers are used to sheer the wool from sheep; some can clip sheep in less than one minute.

READING TIPS

Before Reading

■ To stock the food shelves of supermarkets, farmers use nature and technology to produce a good harvest. However, not all farmers can be so productive, and not all climates produce the same products. This is why trading is important.

■ Discuss the export/import process—how most nations get and receive based on our country's needs. Point out some key import areas on the map: Canada, China, Australia, Brazil, South Africa, Mexico and the Middle East.

■ Sometimes, when we go to war with countries that produce the goods we need, we run the risk of losing our access to those goods. Trade is often tied to politics. Wars risk lives and also may ruin trading relationships.

Critical Thinking

■ What is a good? (An item we use for a purpose.) Find goods around your classroom. (pencils, erasers, desks, chalk, computers, books)

■ Ask: What would happen if we couldn't get goods from one source? Do you think the United States uses more than one source for a good? (The United States has many trading partners.)

■ What kind of goods do you think we get from Mexico? (silver) South Africa? (gold) Asia? (rice) Who exports coffee? (South America) electronics? (Japan)

Activities

■ The word "goods" makes us think of opposites—good and bad, hot and cold, fast and slow. Write down ten opposites, then share them with the class.

■ Rice might make you think of Asia. What other word associations can you think of? (e.g., koalas and Australia; the Eiffel Tower and France; the Empire State Building and New York City; double-decker buses and London, and so on.) Write a word association that deals with school—"When I think of school, I think of _____."

EXTENSION ACTIVITIES

LOOKING AT PHOTOGRAPHS

How do goods get from one part of the world to another?

LEARNING THE RULES

Skills: Current Events, Cognitive Thinking
Curriculum Area: Social Studies

For goods to travel to this country, they have to meet certain standards of quality. They also have to pass strict customs rules and regulations, which exist to protect people's health. The United States doesn't want to run the risk of bringing in diseases or foreign insects that could harm people or the environment. Discuss the rules of passing through customs as a traveler going to another country. Ask if any children have ever been through this process. Have students use construction paper and markers to create their own passports. Discuss what a passport is.

WEIGHTS AND MEASUREMENTS

Skill: Measuring
Curriculum Areas: Math, Social Studies

To receive or send goods, we often need to weigh and measure them. How much you pay for something is often related to how much it costs per pound. Take a class trip to a local supermarket. Visit the fruit and vegetable section. Have children choose a fruit and a vegetable that are priced by pound. First ask: Can you guess how much a pound (of bananas or apples, for instance) would look like? Then invite students to test their guesses by weighing the produce. How close did they come? Can they estimate how much their produce would cost?

ANSWER KEY

READER

Think and Respond **1.** Foods, wool, gold and silver come to the United States from other places. **2.** Goods like bananas come to the United States from far away because that is where they are grown; goods like silver and gold are mined far away and must be shipped to the United States. **3.** Goods from other places give us food, clothing, and natural resources we need. When we buy goods from other places, the money we pay helps those nations.

Write about Goods Children should write a list of goods that come from their town or city. They should include information that tells where the goods are bought.

© Harcourt

Weighing In

How much do you weigh? Sometimes your weight is different in the morning than it is at night. Weigh yourself each morning for 5 days. Do the same each night. Record your weight here. Do you see a difference?

MONDAY Morning_____

Evening_____

TUESDAY Morning_____

Evening_____

WEDNESDAY Morning_____

Evening_____

THURSDAY Morning_____

Evening_____

FRIDAY Morning_____

Evening_____

© Harcourt

Name_____

Label Geography

Many goods are imported into the United States. They may be brought here from as far away as China or as near as Canada or Mexico. Most goods are labeled with the name of the country in which they were made, grown, or packaged. Look for labels and see how many different countries supply goods that you use!

My **sweater** is made in

_____ .

My **notebook** is made in

_____ .

My **favorite toy** is made in

_____ .

My **sneakers** are made in

_____ .

My **favorite fruit** is grown in

_____ .